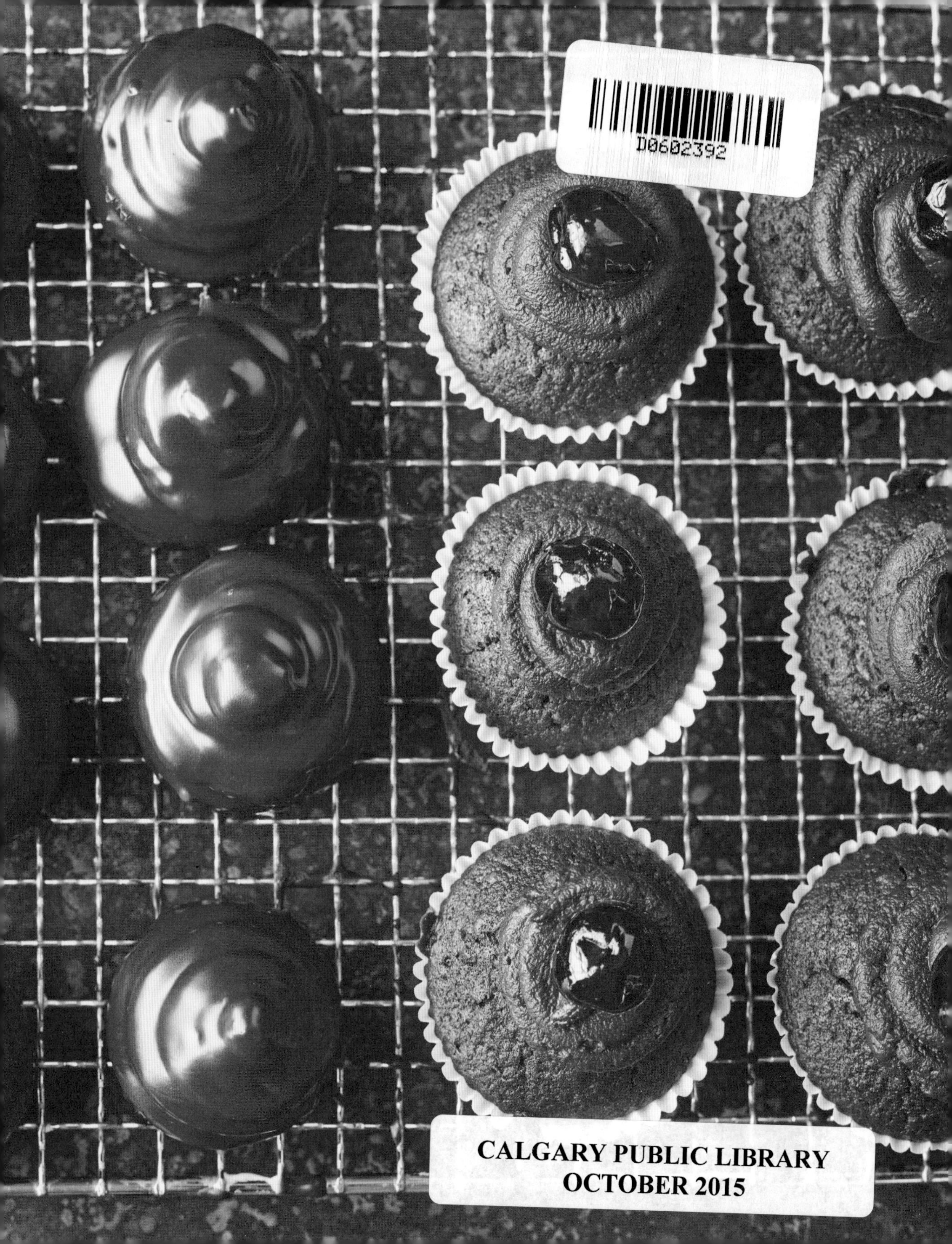

deliciously chocolatey

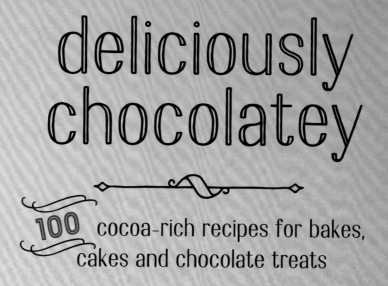

deliciously chocolatey

100 cocoa-rich recipes for bakes, cakes and chocolate treats

Victoria Glass

photography by Dan Jones

RYLAND PETERS & SMALL

LONDON • NEW YORK

Dedication

For Lesley, my wonderful mum.

Designer Maria Lee-Warren
Commissioning Editor Stephanie Milner
Production Manager Gordana Simakovic
Art Director Leslie Harrington
Editorial Director Julia Charles
Publisher Cindy Richards

Prop Stylists Liz Belton and Linda Pullin
Food Stylist Mitzie Wilson
Indexer Hilary Bird

First published in 2015
by Ryland Peters & Small
20–21 Jockey's Fields,
London WC1R 4BW
and
341 E 116th Street
New York, NY 10029
www.rylandpeters.com

10 9 8 7 6 5 4 3 2 1

Text © Victoria Glass 2015

Design and photographs
© Ryland Peters & Small 2015

ISBN: 978-1-84975-657-0

Printed and bound in China

A CIP record for this book is available from the British Library.

US Library of Congress Cataloging-in-Publication Data has been applied for.

Notes

• Both British (Metric) and American (Imperial plus US cups) are included in these recipes for your convenience, however it is important to work with one set of measurements and not alternate between the two within a recipe.

• All spoon measurements are level unless otherwise specified.

• All eggs are medium (UK) or large (US), unless specified as large, in which case US extra-large should be used. Uncooked or partially cooked eggs should not be served to the very old, frail, young children, pregnant women or those with compromised immune systems.

• Ovens should be preheated to the specified temperatures. We recommend using an oven thermometer. If using a fan-assisted oven, adjust temperatures according to the manufacturer's instructions.

• All cake ingredients should be fresh and used at room temperature unless otherwise specified. Take any refrigerated ingredients, such as butter and eggs out of the cold at least 1 hour before you bake.

• Whenever butter is called for within these recipes, unsalted butter should be used unless otherwise specified.

• When a recipe calls for the grated zest of citrus fruit, buy unwaxed fruit and wash well before using. If you can only find treated fruit, scrub well in warm soapy water before using.

• When a recipe calls for full-fat cream cheese, it should be white, creamy smooth and have at least 24 per cent fat content, such as Kraft Philadelphia.

contents

introduction

There is no doubting the myriad charms of chocolate. The Latin for cacao, *Theobroma*, doesn't mean 'food of the gods' for nothing. Indulgent and seductive, chocolate can cheer the darkest of days and even has the added bonus of containing multiple health benefits. Generous levels of magnesium, potassium, copper, iron, phosphorous and calcium can all be found in chocolate and research indicates that cocoa products can actually help to lower blood pressure and alleviate stress.

Sadly, this doesn't give us carte blanche to scoff chocolate pâtisserie with wild abandon, as the addition of butter, cream and sugar undoes most of its natural saintly properties. But a little of what you fancy does you good and there is still some smugness to revel in by enriching your body with nutrients you can't get from other indulgences.

There are few people who can resist the seductive powers of chocolate. The Aztec emperor, Montezuma, was said to guzzle huge quantities of cacao in order to fuel his amorous assignations. Although there is no definitive evidence that chocolate has any magical effects as an aphrodisiac, it does contain two ingredients, which may be partly responsible for its sensual status: tryptophan, a building block of serotonin, a feel-good brain chemical; and phenylethylamine, a stimulant released when you fall in love.

The story of chocolate begins in Mesoamerica, with evidence of the Mokaya people drinking chocolate as far back as 1900 BC. The Mayans established cocoa plantations as early as 600 AD, but it wasn't until the 16th century that Europe was first introduced to chocolate. The Spanish explorer, Hernán Cortés, brought cacao to the Spanish court in 1519 after conquering Mexico. Montezuma himself had given Cortés a cup of spiced chocolate – a great honour indeed, considering the Aztec people valued cacao so much they used it as currency. After adding sugar, the Spanish were so keen to keep their discovery a secret that the rest of Europe was left in a world devoid of chocolate for another 100 years.

Chocolate as we know it today was produced as recently as 1828, when a Dutchman named Casparus Johannes van Houten invented a process of extracting the cocoa butter and cocoa powder from the roasted bean. His son, Coenraad, a chemist, later invented a method of alkalizing the cocoa, known as Dutch processing, which created a milder, less bitter flavour and a more easily used product. Once Casparus' patent ran out, the English company J. S. Fry & Sons produced the first modern chocolate bar in 1847. Switzerland's Daniel Peter added powdered milk to create the first milk chocolate in the mid 1870s, while Rodolphe Lindt went on to take chocolate's development further by introducing the process of conching in 1879, a manufacturing technique of scraping and mixing, resulting in a smoother, better blended product.

Chocolate is a matchless luxury and the epitome of celebration and this book will ensure you have all the delicious chocolate recipes you'll ever need to treat yourself and your loved ones, whatever the occasion.

biscuits and cookies

Dodgers, biscotti, shortbread
and more, all with a
chocolate twist

choco dodgers

250 g/2 sticks soft butter

125 g/²/₃ cup caster/
  granulated sugar

225 g/1³/₄ cups plain/
  all-purpose flour

100 g/³/₄ cup rice flour

50 g/scant ¹/₂ cup cocoa
  powder

a pinch of salt

2 teaspoons vanilla extract

icing/confectioners' sugar,
  for dusting (optional)

Chocolate ganache

100 g/3¹/₂ oz. dark/
  bittersweet chocolate
  (60–70% cocoa solids),
  chopped

100 ml/scant ¹/₂ cup
  single/light cream

1 teaspoon vanilla extract

1 tablespoon light
  muscovado/brown sugar

White chocolate
ganache variation

150 g/5 oz. white
  chocolate, chopped

75 ml/¹/₃ cup double/heavy
  cream

*a 6-cm/2¹/₂-in. scalloped
  edged round cookie cutter*

*a 2.5-cm/1-in. heart-shaped
  cookie cutter*

*1–2 baking sheets lined with
  baking parchment*

*a disposable piping/pastry
  bag*

Makes about 15

These crumbly chocolate shortbread sandwiches, generously filled with chocolate ganache, make a sophisticated alternative to the jam-filled variety.

Cream together the butter and sugar until light and fluffy. Sift in the flours and cocoa powder, and mix together with the salt and vanilla until just combined. Do not overwork the dough or your dodgers will be tough. Wrap the dough in clingfilm/plastic wrap and chill for at least 30 minutes.

In the meantime, make the chocolate (or white chocolate, see below) ganache. Put the chocolate in a heatproof bowl and set aside. Put the cream, vanilla and sugar in a saucepan set over a gentle heat and stir until the sugar has completely dissolved. Increase the heat slightly and allow the cream to just come to the boil. Take it off the heat and leave to stand for 1 minute. Pour the cream over the chocolate and mix with a rubber spatula until it is fully combined and you have a smooth, glossy ganache. Set at room temperature for about an hour, or until thickened but still spreadable. Spoon the ganache into a piping/pastry bag and set aside.

Roll out the dough to thickness of 5 mm/¹/₄ in. and cut out 30 rounds. Cut out a heart from the centre of half of the cookies and arrange on the prepared baking sheets. Bring any scraps together, re-roll and cut out as many cookies as possible from the dough. Chill in the fridge for an hour.

Preheat the oven to 170°C (325°F) Gas 3.

Bake the cookies in the preheated oven for 15–20 minutes. Transfer to a wire rack and leave to cool completely.

Snip the end off the piping/pastry bag and squeeze a generous blob of ganache onto the whole biscuits. Gently press the biscuits with hearts cut out on top to create sandwiches. Dust with icing/confectioners' sugar if you wish.

White chocolate ganache
To make a white chocolate ganache, put the chocolate in a heatproof bowl. Heat the cream until just boiling and leave to cool for about 30 seconds before pouring over the chocolate. Stir with a spatula until all the chocolate has melted and leave to cool completely. Once cold, transfer the ganache to the fridge for a few hours, or until set but not rock hard – it needs to be soft enough to pipe.

chocolate crinkles

These American chocolate cookies are chewy,
fudgy and, best of all, quick and easy to make.

40 g/⅓ cup cocoa powder

135 g/⅔ cup caster/
  granulated sugar

40 ml/3 tablespoons
  sunflower oil

2 eggs

1 teaspoon vanilla extract

100 g/¾ cup plain/
  all-purpose flour

½ teaspoon baking powder

a pinch of salt

25 g/3½ tablespoons
  icing/confectioners' sugar

*a baking sheet lined with
  baking parchment*

Makes about 12

Sift the cocoa into a mixing bowl, add the sugar and oil and whisk together.
Add the eggs, one at a time, followed by the vanilla. Sift in the flour and baking
powder and add the salt, and whisk again until just combined. Wrap the dough
with clingfilm/plastic wrap and chill for at least 4 hours or for up to 2 days.

When ready to bake, preheat the oven to 180°C (350°F) Gas 4.

Sift the icing/confectioners' sugar into a wide bowl. Roll the cookie dough with
your hands into golf-ball sized rounds and roll them in the icing/confectioners'
sugar until coated.

Arrange them on the prepared baking sheet, spaced well apart to allow for
spreading. Bake in the preheated oven for 10–12 minutes and leave to cool for
a few minutes on the baking sheet before transferring to a wire rack to cool
completely before eating.

chocolate and vanilla pinwheels

There's no need to choose between vanilla and
chocolate with my pinwheels. These fun spiral cookies
combine the best of both worlds.

Vanilla dough

125 g/1 stick soft butter
65 g/⅓ cup caster/
   granulated sugar
135 g/1 cup plus 1
   tablespoon plain/
   all-purpose flour
50 g/scant ½ cup rice flour
a pinch of salt
1 teaspoon vanilla extract
½ beaten egg

Chocolate dough

125 g/1 stick soft butter
65 g/⅓ cup caster/
   granulated sugar
115 g/1 scant cup plain/
   all-purpose flour
50 g/scant ½ cup rice flour
25 g/3½ tablespoons cocoa
   powder
a pinch of salt
1 teaspoon vanilla extract
½ beaten egg

a little milk, for brushing

*1–2 baking sheets lined with
   baking parchment*

Makes 30

To make the vanilla dough, cream together the butter and sugar until light and
fluffy. Sift in the flours and salt, and mix together with the vanilla and egg until
just combined. Do not overwork the dough or your pinwheels will be tough.
Wrap the dough in clingfilm/plastic wrap and chill for at least 30 minutes,
or until firm enough to roll.

To make the chocolate dough, cream together the butter and sugar until light
and fluffy. Sift in the flours, cocoa and salt, and mix together with the vanilla
and egg until just combined. Do not overwork the dough or your pinwheels
will be tough. Wrap the dough in clingfilm/plastic wrap and chill for at least
30 minutes, or until firm enough to roll.

Roll both doughs into rectangles with a thickness of 3 mm/⅛ in., each about
18 x 30 cm/7 x 12 in. in size. Brush the chocolate rectangle with a little milk
and place the vanilla rectangle on top. Gently roll again to ensure the two
doughs stick together. Trim away the edges of the rectangles and roll up the
dough tightly like a swiss roll/jellyroll, starting from the long edge. Carefully
wrap the dough roulade in clingfilm/plastic wrap and pop in the fridge for at
least an hour, or until very firm.

Preheat the oven to 170°C (325°F) Gas 3.

Unwrap the dough and use a serrated bread knife to slice it into 1-cm/⅜-in.
thick cookies. If the biscuits are no longer perfectly round after slicing, carefully
reshape them with your hands. Arrange the biscuits on the prepared baking
sheets, spaced well apart to allow for spreading. Brush with a little milk and
bake in the preheated oven for 18–20 minutes, or until firm. Transfer to a wire
rack to cool before eating.

bourbons and tim tams

One of Britain's most popular treats, these chocolate biscuits are sandwiched together with chocolate buttercream. Australian Tim Tams have the addition of malt and are coated in a layer of melted chocolate.

115 g/1 scant cup plain/all-purpose flour
30 g/¼ cup cocoa powder
½ teaspoon bicarbonate of/baking soda
a pinch of salt
65 g/5 tablespoons butter, cut into cubes
50 g/¼ cup light muscovado/brown sugar
2 tablespoons golden/light corn syrup
1–2 tablespoons milk

Chocolate buttercream

50 g/3 tablespoons soft butter
75 g/½ cup icing/confectioners' sugar
1 tablespoon cocoa powder
1 teaspoon vanilla extract
a splash of milk, if needed

Tim Tam top-up (optional)

20 g/3 tablespoons malted milk powder
200 g/6½ oz. milk/semi-sweet chocolate, finely chopped and melted

2 baking sheets lined with baking parchment

Makes 15

Put the flour, cocoa, bicarbonate of/baking soda and salt in a food processor and blitz to combine. Add the butter, sugar and golden/light corn syrup and pulse until the mixture starts coming together. Add the milk, 1 tablespoon at a time, and pulse until the mixture forms a dough. Scoop the dough out onto a sheet of clingfilm/plastic wrap, wrap it up and chill in the fridge for 20 minutes.

Unwrap the dough and roll out on a lightly floured surface to a large rectangle about 3-mm/⅛-in. thick. Trim the edges before cutting 30 rectangles (each about 5 x 3 cm/2 x 1¼ in.). Arrange the biscuits on the prepared baking sheets and pop them in the fridge to chill for 20 minutes.

Preheat the oven to 180°C (350°F) Gas 4.

Use a skewer to prick 8–10 holes (2 rows of 4 or 5) in the biscuits and bake in the preheated oven for 18–20 minutes, or until the biscuits are firm and dry. Transfer to a wire rack to cool completely.

To make the chocolate buttercream, simply whisk the butter until soft and fluffy, sift in half of the icing/confectioners' sugar and whisk again. Sift in the remaining icing/confectioners' sugar and cocoa and whisk until combined. Add the vanilla and a splash of milk to slacken the mixture slightly if needed.

Spread half of the cooled biscuits with a heaped teaspoon of filling before sandwiching them with the remaining biscuits.

Tim Tams

For a Tim Tam variation, add 10 g/1½ tablespoons of malted milk powder to the dough mixture and follow the instructions for baking above. Add the remaining malted milk powder to the chocolate buttercream and sandwich the biscuits together as above. Flash freeze them for 10 minutes to make coating them in melted chocolate easier. Dip the sandwiches in the chocolate until fully coated, tap off the excess and place on a sheet of baking parchment to set.

chocolate macarons

These dainty French confections with a raspberry or espresso filling spell pure elegance and all your friends and family will hail you as a genius for making them yourself.

130 g/1 generous cup ground almonds
170 g/1½ cups icing/confectioners' sugar
50 g/scant ½ cup cocoa powder
150 g/²/₃ cup egg whites (roughly equivalent to 5 egg whites)
a pinch of salt
120 g/scant ²/₃ cup caster/superfine sugar

Raspberry and white chocolate ganache

100 ml/scant ½ cup raspberry purée
150 g/5 oz. white chocolate, chopped
25 g/2 tablespoons butter

Espresso buttercream

100 g/6½ tablespoons soft butter
150 g/1⅓ cups icing/confectioners' sugar
1–2 teaspoons instant espresso powder dissolved in 1 tablespoon boiling water

2–3 piping/pastry bags fitted with a 1-cm/³/₈-in. plain nozzle/tip
1–2 heavy baking sheets lined with baking parchment

Makes 20

First make the raspberry and white chocolate ganache. Heat the raspberry purée until just boiling, leave to cool for about 30 seconds, then pour over the chocolate and butter in a heatproof bowl. Stir until the chocolate and butter have melted and cool completely. Spoon the ganache into one of the piping/pastry bags and chill in the fridge for 6–8 hours, or until set. The ganache will fill 20 macarons or you can make espresso buttercream instead. Whisk the butter until soft and sift in half of the icing/confectioners' sugar. Whisk again before sifting in the remaining half. Add the espresso and whisk well until light and fluffy. Spoon the buttercream into one of the piping/pastry bags and set aside.

To make the macaron shells, put the ground almonds in a food processor and blitz until incredibly fine. Don't leave the motor running for too long though, or the almonds will become oily. Once blitzed, add the icing/confectioners' sugar and cocoa and pulse until fully combined and lump free. Pass the mixture through a fine mesh sieve/strainer two or three times. In a large and spotlessly clean bowl, use a handheld electric whisk to whisk the egg whites with a pinch of salt until stiff. Gradually, a tablespoon at a time, add the caster/superfine sugar, whisking between each addition. You should be left with a shiny and very stiff meringue. Fold the blitzed ingredients into the meringue until fully combined. Continue mixing until the mixture has a soft, dropping consistency. Spoon the mixture into another piping/pastry bag and, with the nozzle/tip pointed straight down, carefully pipe 40 rounds about 3.5 cm/1³/₈ in. in diameter, spaced well apart to allow for spreading. Lift and drop the sheets on a hard surface three times to expel any air bubbles. Set aside for an hour.

Preheat the oven to 180°C (350°F) Gas 4. For best results, turn off the fan – if you can't, reduce the temperature to 160°C (325°F) Gas 3.

Bake the macaron shells in the preheated oven for 16–18 minutes, or until dry and glossy with raised feet. Open the oven door briefly 3 times during cooking, to release any steam. Slide the macaron shells off the baking sheets onto wire cooling racks. Leave to cool completely before carefully peeling the macaron shells off the paper. The shells should lift off the paper easily.

Sandwich two macaron shells together with a generous blob of ganache or espresso buttercream. Once filled, consume within 2–3 days – they are best eaten the day after they are made.

billionaire's shortbread

Millionaire's shortbread is thought to date back to nineteenth-century Scotland, but I've brought it into the twenty-first century by making it even richer. This traybake goes up a financial bracket with chocolate shortbread and a shimmer of edible gold.

200 g/6½ oz. dark/
  bittersweet chocolate
  (60–70% cocoa solids),
  broken into pieces
edible gold lustre, to
  decorate (optional)

Chocolate shortbread

75 g/⅓ cup caster/
  granulated sugar
150 g/1 stick plus 2
  tablespoons soft butter
125 g/1 cup plain/
  all-purpose flour
75 g/⅔ cup rice flour
25 g/3½ tablespoons cocoa
  powder
a pinch of salt
1 teaspoon vanilla extract

Salted caramel

125 g/1 stick butter
75 g/⅓ cup light
  muscovado/brown sugar
25 g/1½ tablespoons
  golden/light corn syrup
1 tablespoon vanilla extract
1 heaped teaspoon salt
a 379-g/14-oz. can
  sweetened condensed milk

a 20-cm/8-in. loose-
  bottomed square cake
  pan, greased and lined
  with baking parchment

Makes 16

First make the chocolate shortbread. Cream together the sugar and butter until light and fluffy. Sift in the flours, cocoa and salt, and mix together with the vanilla until just combined. Do not overwork the dough or your shortbread will be tough. Press the dough into the base of the prepared baking pan with your fingers or the back of a spoon. Chill for 30 minutes.

Preheat the oven to 150°C (300°F) Gas 2.

Bake in the preheated oven for 35–40 minutes, or until firm and dry to the touch. Leave to cool in the pan on top of a wire rack.

Meanwhile, make the salted caramel. Put all the ingredients, except for the condensed milk, into a saucepan and stir continuously over a gentle heat until the butter has melted and the sugar and salt have dissolved. Add the condensed milk and increase the heat, stirring frequently, and being careful not to let the base of the mixture catch. Bring to the boil, still stirring every now and then, until the mixture has thickened and turned a deep golden colour. Take the pan off the heat and leave to cool slightly.

Pour the still-warm salted caramel over the cooled shortbread base and leave to cool completely.

For the topping, put the chocolate in a heatproof bowl suspended over a pan of barely simmering water to melt. Stir every now and then. Once melted, leave to cool slightly before pouring the chocolate over the cold caramel. Leave to cool completely before dusting the top with edible gold lustre, if using, and pushing the base of the pan out. Cut the billionaire's shortbread into 16 even squares or alternatively, for larger portions, you can cut it into 8 bars.

chocolate and hazelnut biscotti

These twice-baked Italian biscuits hail from the city of Prato in Tuscany. The first documented recipe is centuries old, but the version we know and love today is based on the work by nineteenth-century pâtissier, Antonio Mattei. Delicious dunked in a steaming espresso or glass of Vin Santo, they can be stored in an airtight container for at least a fortnight.

115 g/1 scant cup plain/
 all-purpose flour
1 teaspoon baking powder
a pinch of salt
80 g/⅓ cup plus
 1 tablespoon caster/
 granulated sugar
1 egg, beaten
100 g/⅔ cup blanched
 and roasted hazelnuts,
 roughly chopped
100 g/⅔ cup dark/
 bittersweet chocolate chips

*1–2 baking sheets lined with
 baking parchment*

Makes about 24

Preheat the oven to 180°C (350°F) Gas 4.

Sift the flour and baking powder into a large bowl and stir in the salt and sugar. Stir in the egg until the mixture begins to come together, then knead to form a dough. The mixture will be dry at first, but keep gently kneading until you get a smooth consistency. Add the nuts and chocolate chips and work them into the dough until evenly distributed.

Turn the dough out onto a lightly floured surface and divide into two pieces. Using lightly floured hands, roll the dough into two sausages. Arrange the sausages on one of the prepared baking sheets, spaced well apart to allow for spreading.

Bake in the preheated oven for 25 minutes, or until the dough has risen, spread and feels firm to the touch. Take the sheet out of the oven and transfer the dough to a wire rack to cool for 5 minutes, or until cool enough to handle.

Reduce the oven temperature to 140°C (275°F) Gas 1.

Using a serrated bread knife, cut the dough into slices about 1-cm/⅜-in. thick on the diagonal, then lay them flat on the baking sheets. Bake for a further 15 minutes, turn over, then bake for another 15 minutes, or until dry and golden. Transfer the biscotti to a wire rack to cool completely.

samoas

Vanilla cookies topped with toasted coconut and caramel and drizzled with dark/bittersweet chocolate. With this recipe based on Samoas in your repertoire, you can enjoy Girl Scout Cookies all year round.

125 g/1 stick soft butter
65 g/⅓ cup caster/ granulated sugar
135 g/1 cup plus 1 tablespoon plain/ all-purpose flour
50 g/⅓ cup plus 1 tablespoon rice flour
a pinch of salt
1 teaspoon vanilla extract
200 g/6½ oz. dark/ bittersweet chocolate (60–70% cocoa solids), melted

Coconut caramel

175 g/1⅓ cups desiccated/ shredded coconut
125 g/⅔ cup caster/ granulated sugar
75 ml/⅓ cup golden/light corn syrup
¼ teaspoon salt
100 ml/scant ½ cup double/heavy cream
75 ml/⅓ cup sweetened condensed milk
30 g/2 tablespoons butter
1 teaspoon vanilla extract

a 6-cm/2¼-in. round cookie cutter
a 2.5-cm/1-in. round cookie cutter
2–3 baking sheets lined with baking parchment

Makes about 15

Cream together the butter and sugar until light and fluffy. Sift in the flours and salt, and mix together with the vanilla until just combined. Do not overwork the dough or your cookies will be tough. Wrap the dough in clingfilm/plastic wrap and chill for at least 30 minutes.

Roll out the dough on a lightly floured surface to a thickness of 5 mm/¼ in. and cut out rounds using the larger cookie cutter. Cut out a hole in the centre of the biscuits, using the smaller cutter and arrange the biscuits on the prepared baking sheets. Bring any scraps together, re-roll and cut out as many cookies as possible from the dough. Chill in the fridge for an hour.

Preheat the oven to 170°C (325°F) Gas 3.

Bake in the preheated oven for 15–20 minutes, or until pale golden. Transfer the cookies to a wire rack to cool completely. Leave the oven on.

In the meantime, spread the coconut on a clean baking sheet lined with baking parchment and toast, turning once, in the oven for 10 minutes until golden.

To make the caramel, put the sugar, syrup, salt, cream, condensed milk, butter and vanilla in a saucepan set over a gentle heat and stir until the sugar has completely dissolved. Increase the heat and, without stirring, bring to the boil. Reduce the heat and leave to simmer for about 5 minutes, or until the caramel is nice and thick. Carefully spoon about a quarter of the caramel into a heatproof bowl and set aside for later. Stir the coconut into the remaining caramel and set aside until cool enough to touch.

Place the heatproof bowl with the remaining caramel over a pan of barely simmering water and warm through until it has melted enough to spread over the tops of the cold cookies. Spread the cookies with the warmed caramel then press a neat ring of coconut caramel on top. Leave to set.

Dunk the bases of the cookies in the melted chocolate, tap off any excess and place on a sheet of baking parchment to set. Drizzle the remaining chocolate over the tops of the cookies in a zigzag pattern and leave to set.

white choc and nut cookies

———————●———————

Who can resist a soft, chewy, buttery cookie dunked in a glass of ice-cold milk or steaming cup of tea? Here I give you double choc chip for decadent days when only dark/bittersweet chocolate will do and white chocolate and macadamia for days that require extra sweetness.

125 g/1 stick soft butter

75 g/⅓ cup packed light brown sugar

75 g/⅓ cup caster/granulated sugar

1 egg

2 teaspoons vanilla extract

250 g/2 cups plain/all-purpose flour

1 teaspoon bicarbonate of/baking soda

½ teaspoon salt

175 g/1¼ cups white chocolate chips

150 g/1 cup macadamia nuts, roughly chopped

Double choc chip cookie variation

50 g/scant ½ cup cocoa powder

175 g/1¼ cups milk/semi-sweet chocolate chips

2 baking sheets lined with baking parchment

Makes about 20

Cream together the butter and sugars until just combined. Beat in the egg, followed by the vanilla. Sift in the flour and bicarbonate of/baking soda, then mix in. Fold in the white chocolate chips and macadamia nuts. Wrap the dough in clingfilm/plastic wrap and chill in the fridge for at least 2 hours.

Preheat the oven to 180°C (350°F) Gas 4.

Roll the cookie dough with your hands into golf-ball sized rounds and space them well apart on the prepared baking sheets. Slightly flatten each ball with a palette knife, then bake in the preheated oven for 12–15 minutes, or until slightly golden. Transfer them to a wire rack to cool before eating.

Double choc chip cookies

To make double choc chip cookies, follow the instructions above using 50 g/⅓ cup less plain/all-purpose flour, adding cocoa to the dough mixture and replacing the white chocolate and macadamia nuts with milk/semi-sweet chocolate chips.

small cakes and bakes

Friands, traybakes,
madeleines and scones,
given a cocoa boost

chocolate teacakes

A shiny shell of chocolate hiding a fluffy cloud of either orange blossom or peppermint marshmallow on a crisp chocolate biscuit base, these teacakes are a real treat.

35 g/3 tablespoons caster/
  granulated sugar
80 g/²/₃ cup plain/
  all-purpose flour
15 g/2 tablespoons cocoa
  powder
a pinch of salt
65 g/5 tablespoons soft
  butter
2 tablespoons milk
250 g/8 oz. dark/
  bittersweet chocolate
  (60–70% cocoa solids),
  chopped

Filling

2 large egg whites
125 g/²/₃ cup caster/
  granulated sugar
¼ teaspoon cream of tartar
1 teaspoon orange blossom
  water (or a few drops of
  peppermint extract)

*a baking sheet lined with
  baking parchment
a 6-cm/2¼-in. round cookie
  cutter
a chocolate thermometer
a 6-hole (7-cm/3-in.) silicone
  sphere chocolate mould
an electric whisk (optional)
a disposable piping/pastry
  bag*

Makes 6

First make the biscuit base. Put the sugar, flour, cocoa and salt in a food processor and blitz to combine. Add the butter and blitz again until the mixture resembles fine breadcrumbs. Finally, add the milk and pulse until the mixture forms a dough. Wrap in clingfilm/plastic wrap and chill for 20 minutes.

Roll the dough out on a lightly floured surface to a thickness of 3 mm/⅛ in., then, use the cookie cutter to cut out 6 rounds. Arrange the biscuits on the prepared baking sheet and return to the fridge for another 20 minutes.

Preheat the oven to 180°C (350°F) Gas 4.

Bake the biscuits in the preheated oven for 15–18 minutes, or until firm and dry to the touch. Transfer to a wire rack to cool.

Temper the chocolate by melting two-thirds of it in a heatproof bowl set over a pan of barely simmering water until it reaches 45°C (113°F). Remove the bowl from the heat, gradually add the remaining chocolate and gently stir until the chocolate cools to 27°C (81°F). At this stage, return the bowl to the heat, gently stir and reheat until the chocolate reaches 31°C (88°F).

Generously coat the insides of the chocolate mould with the tempered chocolate and set aside at room temperature. Dunk the cooled biscuits in the remaining chocolate, tap off any excess and leave to set on a sheet of baking parchment.

To make the filling, whisk everything except for the orange blossom water (or peppermint extract, if preferred) in a large heatproof bowl set over a pan of barely simmering water, until the sugar has dissolved and the egg whites are warm. Take the bowl off the heat and continue to whisk until very stiff and glossy. This can take several minutes, so use an electric whisk if you have one, and be patient. Whisk in the orange blossom water (or peppermint extract). Spoon the mixture into the piping/pastry bag.

Snip the end off the piping/pastry bag and fill the chocolate half spheres three-quarters full. Place the chocolate-coated biscuits on top and gently press down. Use any remaining tempered chocolate to seal the edges. Leave the teacakes to set at room temperature before carefully turning out. Eat immediately.

orange and chocolate chip madeleines

———◆———◇———◆———

Romanticized in the 'episode of the madeleine' in Proust's
In Search of Lost Time for their connection with
involuntary memory, these shell-shaped French cakes
are undeniably evocative. I've added chocolate chips and
fragrant orange zest or you can make them richer with
a dollop of peanut butter, following the instructions below.

100 g/½ cup caster/
  granulated sugar
2 eggs
100 g/6½ tablespoons
  butter, melted and cooled
  slightly
100 g/¾ cup plain/
  all-purpose flour
a pinch of salt
1 teaspoon baking powder
finely grated zest and freshly
  squeezed juice of 1 orange
50 g/⅓ cup dark/
  bittersweet chocolate chips
icing/confectioners' sugar,
  to dust (optional)

Peanut butter
madeleine variation

2 tablespoons smooth
  peanut butter
75 g/½ cup dark/
  bittersweet chocolate chips

*a 12-shell madeleine sheet,
  greased and lightly dusted
  with flour*

Makes 12

Whisk together the sugar and eggs until combined, light and frothy. Add the butter and salt, sift in the flour and baking powder and lightly whisk to combine. Stir through the orange zest and juice and fold in the chocolate chips. Set the batter aside to rest for at least 30 minutes, but preferably for as long as 3 hours. You can leave the batter covered in the fridge for up to 2 days.

Preheat the oven to 200°C (375°F) Gas 5.

Pour the batter into the prepared madeleine sheet and bake in the preheated oven for 8–10 minutes, or until each madeleine is slightly golden and well risen in the centre.

Once the cakes have cooled enough to touch, transfer them to a wire rack to cool. Dust with icing/confectioners' sugar, if you wish, and serve. Madeleines are best eaten on the day they are baked.

Peanut butter madeleines

For a peanut butter variation of these madeleines, add the peanut butter with the butter as above and omit the orange zest and juice. Increase the amount of chocolate chips for extra indulgence.

bacon, maple and pecan brownies

◆————◆————◆

The heady combination of salt and sweet makes my
bacon, maple and pecan brownies irresistibly seductive.
Or, for a meat-free alternative, try my umami-rich and
gloriously sticky chocolate and miso caramel variation.

12 rashers/slices smoked
    streaky bacon, finely
    chopped
75 g/¼ cup maple syrup
250 g/8 oz. dark/
    bittersweet chocolate
    (60–70% cocoa solids),
    broken into pieces
250 g/2 sticks butter
125 g/⅔ cup light
    muscovado/brown sugar
125 g/⅔ cup caster/
    granulated sugar
4 eggs, beaten
a pinch of salt
100 g/¾ cup plain/
    all-purpose flour
½ teaspoon baking powder
½ teaspoon bicarbonate of/
    baking soda
100 g/⅔ cup pecans,
    roughly chopped

**Miso caramel
variation**

175 g/¾ cup plus
    2 tablespoons caster/
    granulated sugar
125 ml/½ cup double/
    heavy cream
2 tablespoons white miso
2 teaspoons vanilla extract

*a 20 x 25-cm/8 x 10-in.
cake pan, greased and
lined with baking
parchment*

Makes 16

Preheat the oven to 170°C (325°F) Gas 3.

First, dry fry the bacon in a frying pan/skillet set over a medium heat until golden. Stir in the maple syrup, turn off the heat and set aside to cool in the pan.

Put the chocolate and butter in a large heatproof bowl suspended over a pan of barely simmering water. Stir every now and then, until all the ingredients have melted. Take the bowl off the heat and leave to cool slightly before whisking in the sugars, bacon syrup, eggs and salt. Sift in the flour and raising agents, and fold in together with the pecans.

Pour the mixture into the prepared cake pan and bake in the preheated oven for 25–30 minutes, or until just set. An inserted skewer should still have a little stickiness left on it. Remove from the oven and let cool in the pan on top of a wire rack before turning out and cutting into squares.

Chocolate brownies with miso caramel

For a miso caramel variation or these brownies, omit the bacon, maple syrup and pecans and begin by making the caramel. Put the sugar and 70 ml/⅓ cup of water in a saucepan set over a gentle heat and stir until the sugar has dissolved. Stop stirring, increase the heat and bring the syrup to the boil. Use a wet pastry brush to wash down any sugar crystals that stick to the side of the pan. When the sugar turns deep amber, remove from the heat and carefully pour in the cream. The mixture will bubble up, but whisk well to mix. If the cold cream causes the caramel to harden too much, pop it back over a gentle heat until it melts again. Whisk in the miso and set aside.

As above, make the brownie mixture but add vanilla with the salt.

Pour the mixture into the prepared cake pan and level the top with a palette knife. Drizzle over half of the miso caramel. If the miso caramel has hardened, gently heat it to soften it again. Use a skewer to swirl the caramel around and bake as above.

Remove from the oven and immediately drizzle the rest of the caramel over the top. Let cool in the pan, turn out and cut as above.

miracles

These simple chocolate fairy cakes hail from New Zealand
and make perfect lunchbox and bake sale fare.

130 ml/½ cup milk
2 tablespoons golden/light
    corn syrup
100 g/½ cup light
    muscovado/brown sugar
60 g/½ stick butter
a pinch of bicarbonate of/
    baking soda
2 eggs, beaten
170 g/1⅓ cups self-raising/
    rising flour
30 g/¼ cup cocoa powder
3 tablespoons raspberry
    jam/jelly
12 natural glacé/candied
    cherries

Buttercream

75 g/5 tablespoons soft
    butter
75 g/2½ oz. dark/
    bittersweet chocolate
    (60–70% cocoa solids),
    melted and cooled
100 g/1 scant cup icing/
    confectioners' sugar
a splash of milk, if needed

a 12-hole muffin pan lined
    with paper cases
a piping/pastry bag fitted
    with a plain nozzle/tip

Makes 12

Preheat the oven to 180°C (350°F) Gas 4.

Put the milk, golden/light corn syrup, sugar and butter in a large saucepan set over a medium heat and stir until melted. Take the pan off the heat and whisk in the bicarbonate of/baking soda. The mixture will foam up slightly. Leave to cool for a few minutes before whisking in the beaten egg. Sift in the flour and cocoa, and fold in until fully incorporated.

Divide the mixture between the paper cases and bake in the preheated oven for 10–15 minutes, or until an inserted skewer comes out clean. Transfer the cakes to a wire rack to cool completely.

Use a small, sharp knife to cut out a small inverted cone shape from the top of each cake. Fill each cavity with jam/jelly before replacing the cut cake tops.

To make the buttercream, simply whisk the butter until very soft before adding the chocolate and whisking to combine. Sift in the icing/confectioners' sugar and whisk until light and fluffy. You can add a splash of milk to slightly slacken the mixture if needed.

Spoon the buttercream into the piping/pastry bag and pipe a swirl of buttercream on top of each cake. Top with a glacé/candied cherry and enjoy.

55 g/½ stick soft butter

55 g/¼ cup light muscovado/brown sugar

1 large egg, beaten

1 teaspoon vanilla extract

40 g/⅓ cup self-raising/ rising flour, sifted

15 g/2 tablespoons cocoa powder, sifted

a pinch of baking powder

a pinch of salt

Buttercream

25 g/2 tablespoons soft butter

25 g/1 oz. dark/bittersweet chocolate (60–70% cocoa solids), melted and cooled

35 g/⅓ cup icing/ confectioners' sugar, sifted

a splash of whole milk, if needed

Coating

100 g/3½ oz. milk/ semi-sweet chocolate, melted and cooled

100 g/3½ oz. white chocolate, melted and cooled

35 g/1 oz. chocolate-covered popping candy/pop rocks

a 15-cm/6-in. shallow cake pan, greased and base-lined with baking parchment

a baking sheet lined with baking parchment

12 lollipop sticks

Makes 12

popping cake pops

These lollipop-sized treats won't fail to delight with the crackle and fizz of their popping candy/pop rocks topping.

Preheat the oven to 180°C (350°F) Gas 4.

To make the cake, simply put all the ingredients in a large mixing bowl and, using a handheld electric whisk, whisk together for a minute or two until you have a soft dropping consistency. Spoon the mixture into the prepared cake pan, level the top with a palette knife and bake in the preheated oven for 15–20 minutes, or until an inserted skewer comes out clean. Leave the cake to cool in its pan for 10 minutes set atop a wire rack, before turning out and leaving to cool completely.

To make the buttercream, simply whisk the butter until very soft before adding the chocolate and whisking to combine. Sift in half of the icing/confectioners' sugar and whisk to combine before adding the remaining icing/confectioners' sugar and whisking until light and fluffy. You can add a splash of milk to slightly slacken the mixture if needed.

Crumble the cooled cake into a mixing bowl until it resembles breadcrumbs and mix in enough buttercream for the mixture to come together to form a sort of dough. You may not need all the buttercream. Pop the mixture in the fridge for 30 minutes, but no longer or it will be too stiff to shape.

Divide the mixture into 12 equal-sized pieces and roll each one between your palms to create smooth spheres. Arrange them on the prepared baking sheet and return to the fridge for at least an hour to set.

Put the popping candy/pop rocks in a shallow bowl and set aside. Starting with the melted milk/semi-sweet chocolate, dunk the tip of a lollipop stick into the chocolate and press it into one of the cake balls. Repeat with five more sticks and balls. Holding the end of the sticks, coat each cake pop with the milk/semi-sweet chocolate until completely covered. Tap off any excess and dip the top of each pop into the popping candy. Insert the base of the lollipop sticks into a piece of Styrofoam and leave to set. Repeat with the second half of the cake balls, this time covering them in the melted white chocolate before dipping them in popping candy. Once set, remove the pops from the foam holder and stand in decorative glass jars to serve.

jaffa cakes

75 g/5 tablespoons soft
butter

85 g/scant ½ cup caster/
granulated sugar

1 egg

150 g/1 cup plus
3 tablespoons plain/
all-purpose flour

½ teaspoon bicarbonate
of/baking soda

a pinch of salt

finely grated zest of ½
orange

85 ml/⅓ cup buttermilk

Orange filling

finely grated zest of 2½
oranges and freshly
squeezed juice of 3

3 tablespoons strained
apricot jam/jelly

3 tablespoons Cointreau
(or other orange liqueur)

2 tablespoons caster/
granulated sugar

4 leaves of gelatine,
soaked in cold water
for at least 10 minutes
(or 2 teaspoons
gelatine powder)

Coating

300 g/10 oz. dark/
bittersweet chocolate
(60–70% cocoa solids),
finely chopped

*a large disposable
piping/pastry bag*

*2 baking sheets lined with
baking parchment*

*a 23 x 33-cm/9 x 13-in.
shallow baking dish lined
with clingfilm/plastic wrap*

*a 5-cm/2-in. round cookie
cutter*

Makes 35

Despite looking more like biscuits, jaffa cakes were officially classified as cakes after a tax argument in a UK court. Whatever they are, there's no denying these chocolate and orange treats are irresistibly delicious and never more so than when homemade.

Preheat the oven to 180°C (350°F) Gas 4.

Cream together the butter and sugar and whisk in the egg. In a separate bowl, sift together the flour, bicarbonate of/baking soda and salt. Stir the orange zest into the buttermilk in a pouring jug/pitcher. Whisk one-third of the dry ingredients into the butter and sugar mixture, then one-third of the orange and buttermilk. Repeat until all the ingredients are fully incorporated. Spoon the mixture into the piping/pastry bag and set aside to rest for 30 minutes.

Snip the end off the piping/pastry bag and pipe 35 rounds, each about 5 cm/ 2 in., onto the prepared baking sheets, spaced well apart to allow for spreading. Bake in the preheated oven for 12–15 minutes, or until the cakes are a pale golden colour. Transfer to a wire rack to cool.

To make the orange filling, put the orange zest and juice, apricot jam/jelly, Cointreau and sugar in a saucepan and stir over a gentle heat until the jam/jelly has melted and the mixture is hot. Take the saucepan off the heat. Squeeze out as much water from the gelatine leaves as you can and whisk into the hot liquid. Pour the mixture into the prepared baking dish – it should be about 3 mm/ ⅛ in. deep. Leave to cool at room temperature before putting in the fridge to set fully.

Next, temper the chocolate by melting two-thirds of it in a heatproof bowl set over a pan of barely simmering water until it reaches 45°C (113°F). Remove the bowl from the heat, gradually add the remaining chocolate and gently stir until the chocolate cools to 27°C (81°F). At this stage, return the bowl to the heat, gently stir and reheat until the chocolate reaches 31°C (88°F). You can, if you wish, simply melt the chocolate and leave it to cool slightly before using (you don't want it to melt the filling!), but the tops won't be shiny.

To assemble, place the cakes on a wire rack, flat side up. Use the cookie cutter to cut out 35 discs of orange filling and use a small palette knife to transfer a disc on top of each cake. Spoon some tempered chocolate over each jaffa cake and smooth their tops with the palette knife. Leave to set before eating.

sarah bernhardt cakes

◆━━━━━━━◆━━━━━━━◆

These elegant cakes are named after the French actress,
Sarah Bernhardt, from the Belle Epoque era.

100 g/²/₃ cup ground
  almonds
100 g/1 scant cup icing/
  confectioners' sugar
75 g/¹/₄ cup (about 2 large)
  egg whites
100 g/¹/₂ cup caster/
  superfine sugar
a tiny pinch of salt

Filling

150 g/5 oz. dark/
  bittersweet chocolate
  (60–70% cocoa solids),
  finely chopped
150 ml/²/₃ cup double/
  heavy cream
40 g/3 tablespoons light
  muscovado/brown sugar
100 g/6¹/₂ tablespoons
  butter, cut into small cubes
2 tablespoons Disaronno
  Amaretto (or other almond
  liqueur)

Glaze

275 g/10 oz. dark/
  bittersweet chocolate,
  chopped
150 g/1 stick plus
  2 tablespoons butter
2 tablespoons golden/light
  corn syrup

a sugar thermometer
2 piping/pastry bags fitted
  with plain 1-cm/³/₈ in.
  nozzles/tips
1–2 baking sheets lined with
  baking parchment

Makes 24

Put the ground almonds in a food processor and blitz until incredibly fine. Don't leave the motor running for too long though, or the almonds will become oily. Add the icing/confectioners' sugar and pulse until fully combined and lump-free. Pass the mixture through a fine mesh sieve/strainer twice. Add half the egg whites (weigh them for accuracy) and mix to form a smooth paste.

Put 80 g/6 tablespoons of the caster/superfine sugar in a small saucepan with 25 ml/1¹/₂ tablespoons of water and heat gently until all the sugar has dissolved. Increase the heat and, without stirring, bring to 118°C (325°F).

In the meantime, put the remaining egg whites in a spotlessly clean bowl with the salt and whisk until stiff. Gradually add the remaining 20 g/2 tablespoons of caster/superfine sugar, whisking between each addition to make a meringue.

Drizzle the hot syrup into the meringue, whisking gently all the time. Once all the syrup has been added, whisk vigorously for 30 seconds until thick and glossy. Fold the meringue into the almond paste in three stages with a spatula. An imprint made with the spatula should disappear in around 15 seconds. Spoon the mixture into one of the piping/pastry bags and pipe rounds, each about 5 cm/2 in., onto the prepared baking sheets, spaced well apart to allow for spreading. Tap the sheets on a hard surface two or three times and set aside to dry out for at least 30 minutes. Preheat the oven to 170°C (325°F) Gas 3.

Bake the macarons in the preheated oven for 12–15 minutes, opening the oven door twice during cooking to release steam. They should feel dry to the touch and have raised feet. Slide the macaron shells off the baking sheets onto wire cooling racks. Cool completely before carefully peeling the shells off the paper.

To make the filling, put all of the ingredients, except for the Disaronno Amaretto, in a pan and stir over a gentle heat until melted. Pour into a large mixing bowl and stir in the Disaronno Amaretto. Once cool, chill for at least 2 hours to set. Whisk the filling until thick and fluffy – the aeration will turn the filling several shades lighter. Spoon into the other piping/pastry bag and pipe tall mounds on top of the macaron shells. Pop them in the fridge or freezer to set firm.

In the meantime, make the glaze by heating all the ingredients in a heatproof bowl suspended over a pan of barely simmering water. Stir until everything has completely melted. Leave to cool, then dunk the piped macarons in the glaze so they are evenly covered right down to the base, turn upright and leave to set.

125 g/scant 1 cup icing/
   confectioners' sugar, plus
   extra for dusting
25 g/2½ tablespoons cocoa
   powder
85 g/¾ cup desiccated/
   shredded coconut
4 egg whites
a pinch of salt
100 g/scant ½ cup coconut
   oil (plus extra for
   greasing), melted and
   cooled
icing/confectioners' sugar,
   to dust

**White chocolate and
chai variation**

85 g/¾ cup ground
   almonds
½ teaspoon each of ground
   ginger and cinnamon
¼ teaspoon each of ground
   cardamom and black
   pepper
⅛ teaspoon ground cloves
100 g/7 tablespoons butter
   (plus extra for greasing),
   melted and cooled
100 g/⅔ cup white
   chocolate chips

*an 8-hole friand pan (or
   muffin pan), greased and
   set on a baking sheet*

Makes 8

friands

These delicious little cakes are light and fluffy.
The dark/bittersweet chocolate and coconut recipe
makes for a stunning gluten- and dairy-free treat, whilst
the warming spices cut through the nursery sweetness
of the white chocolate and chai variation.

Preheat the oven to 180°C (350°F) Gas 4.

Sift together the icing/confectioners' sugar and cocoa in a large mixing bowl.
Stir in the desiccated/shredded coconut.

In a separate bowl, whisk the egg whites and salt to very soft peaks. Make a
well in the middle of the dry ingredients and pour in the whisked egg mixture
and coconut oil and lightly mix to form a batter.

Pour the batter into the friand holes and bake in the preheated oven for
15–20 minutes, or until an inserted skewer comes out clean. Leave to cool in
the pan for 5–10 minutes before transferring to a wire rack to cool completely.

Once cold, dust with icing/confectioners' sugar and serve.

White chocolate and chai friands

For a spiced version of these delicious cakes, omit the cocoa, replace the
dessicated/shredded coconut with ground almonds and add ground ginger,
cinnamon, cardamom, pepper and cloves to the icing/confectioners' sugar.
Replace the coconut oil with melted butter and fold white chocolate chips into
the batter before pouring into the friand pan. Bake as above.

rocky road

· · · · · · · · · · ● · · · · · · · ·

A speedy lunchbox treat that requires no baking at all.
You can add your own twist with extra nuts, different
dried fruits or even some smashed pieces of honeycomb.

200 g/6½ oz. milk/
semi-sweet chocolate,
broken into pieces
200 g/6½ oz. dark/
bittersweet chocolate
(60–70% cocoa solids),
broken into pieces
175 g/1½ sticks butter, cut
into cubes
75 g/⅓ cup golden/light
corn syrup
200 g/6½ oz. Rich Tea
biscuits, smashed into bits
200 g/3 cups mini
marshmallows
icing/confectioners' sugar,
for dusting

Tiffin variation
200 g/6½ oz. digestive
biscuits/graham crackers,
smashed into bits
100 g/⅔ cup glacé/candied
cherries, drained and cut
in half
100 g/⅔ cup (dark) raisins
120 g/4 oz. Maltesers/
Whoppers, lightly smashed

a 20-cm/8-in. square cake
pan lined with baking
parchment
an oiled palette knife

Makes 16

Put the chocolates, butter and golden/light corn syrup in a heatproof bowl
suspended over a pan of barely simmering water. Stir every now and then until
everything has melted. Remove the bowl from the heat and stir in the biscuit bits
and marshmallows.

Pour the mixture into the prepared pan and use the palette knife to smooth over
the top. Once cool, pop it in the fridge to set for at least 2 hours.

Dust the top with icing/confectioners' sugar, remove from the pan and pull
the sides of the baking parchment down before slicing the rocky road into
16 bite-sized squares.

Tiffin
Similar to rocky road, no-bake tiffin bites can be made following the instructions
above but substituting Rich Tea biscuit bits and marshmallows with digestive
biscuit/graham cracker bits, cherries, raisins and Maltesers/Whoppers.

white chocolate and blueberry blondies

Blondies are white chocolate brownies. Squidgy, sticky
white chocolate squares of cake studded with blueberries
make the perfect afternoon pick-you-up, or why not try
a warming hit of wasabi to tingle your taste buds instead.

250 g/8 oz. white chocolate,
  melted and cooled
250 g/2 sticks soft butter
250 g/1¼ cups caster/
  granulated sugar
4 eggs
165 g/1⅓ cups plain/
  all-purpose flour
a pinch of salt
100 g/⅔ cup macadamia
  nuts, roughly chopped
  (optional)
150 g/1½ cups fresh
  blueberries

**White chocolate
and wasabi
blondie variation**

2 tablespoons wasabi paste

*a 20 x 25-cm/8 x 10-in.
cake pan, greased and
lined with baking
parchment*

Makes 16

Preheat the oven to 170°C (325°F) Gas 3.

Cream the butter and sugar together until light and fluffy. Whisk in the eggs,
one at a time. If the mixture begins to curdle, add a tablespoon or two of the
flour. Once all the eggs have been added, whisk in the cool melted chocolate.
Fold in the remaining flour and salt, followed by the nuts (if using) and
blueberries, until the batter is evenly studded.

Pour the batter into the prepared pan and bake in the preheated oven for
25–30 minutes, or until an inserted skewer comes out just clean. Leave to cool
in the pan on top of a wire rack for 10 minutes, before turning out and cutting
into 16 squares. Blondies are delicious eaten warm or cold.

White chocolate and wasabi blondies
For a wasabi variation of these blondies, leave out the nuts and blueberries
and add the wasabi paste once all the eggs have been added.

chocolate fudge cupcakes

— ◦ —

Rich, but extremely light and moist, these cupcakes are a real crowd pleaser.

110 g/½ cup light muscovado/brown sugar

2 tablespoons golden/light corn syrup

55 g/4 tablespoons butter, melted

55 ml/¼ cup sunflower oil

2 eggs, beaten

110 ml/scant ½ cup milk

1 teaspoon vanilla extract

75 g/5 tablespoons dark/bittersweet chocolate, melted and cooled

130 g/1 cup self-raising/rising flour

20 g/2½ tablespoons cocoa powder

½ teaspoon bicarbonate of/baking soda

a small pinch of salt

Fudge topping

125 g/1 stick soft butter

215 g/2 cups icing/confectioners' sugar

125 g/4 oz. dark/bittersweet chocolate, melted and cooled

a splash of milk, if needed

Hot chocolate cupcake variation

25 g/1 oz. dark/bittersweet chocolate, chopped

25 g/2 tablespoons golden/light corn syrup

25 ml/2 tablespoons double/heavy cream

2 egg whites

65 g/⅓ cup caster/granulated sugar

a pinch of cream of tartar

1 teaspoon vanilla extract

mini marshmallows, to decorate (optional)

a 12-hole muffin pan lined with paper cases

a piping/pastry bag fitted with a star nozzle/tip

Preheat the oven to 180°C (350°F) Gas 4.

Whisk together the sugar, syrup, butter, oil, eggs, milk, vanilla and melted chocolate. Sift in the flour, cocoa, bicarbonate of/baking soda and salt and fold until completely incorporated. Fill the paper cases two-thirds of the way up and bake in the preheated oven for 20 minutes, or until an inserted skewer comes out clean. Transfer the cakes onto a wire rack to cool.

To make the fudge topping, whisk the butter for a few seconds until pale and creamy. Sift in half of the icing/confectioners' sugar and whisk to combine. Add the melted chocolate and whisk through before sifting in the remaining icing/confectioners' sugar. Whisk for a minute or so, or until the topping is really creamy and soft. You can add a splash of milk to slightly slacken the mixture if you need to. Spoon the topping into the piping/pastry bag and pipe a generous swirl of buttercream on top of each cooled cake.

Hot chocolate cupcakes

For a hot chocolate variation, bake the cupcakes as above with the addition of a gooey filling and marshmallow topping instead of fudge.

To make the filling, melt the chocolate, syrup and cream together in a small saucepan set over a gentle heat, stirring all the time. Leave to cool, then once the cakes are cool, cut a small cone-shaped hollow out of the centre of each one using a small, sharp knife and fill each hole with the gooey filling.

To make the marshmallow topping, whisk everything except for the vanilla in a large heatproof bowl set over a pan of barely simmering water, until the sugar has dissolved and the egg whites are warm. Take the bowl off the heat and continue to whisk until stiff and glossy. This can take several minutes, so use an electric whisk if you have one and be patient.

Once ready, whisk in the vanilla and pipe the topping onto the cakes as above. Decorate with a scattering of mini marshmallows, if you wish.

Makes 12

double chocolate chip muffins

Light, fluffy and studded with chocolate chips, these
muffins are a cinch to make and even easier to eat.

250 ml/1 cup buttermilk
100 g/6½ tablespoons
  butter, melted and cooled
  slightly
1 large egg, beaten
200 g/1⅔ cups plain/
  all-purpose flour
50 g/scant ½ cup cocoa
  powder
1 teaspoon baking powder
1 teaspoon bicarbonate of/
  baking soda
200 g/1 cup caster/
  granulated sugar
a pinch of salt
150 g/¾ cup dark/
  bittersweet or milk/
  semi-sweet chocolate chips
  (or a mixture of the two)

a 12-hole muffin pan lined
  with paper cases

Makes 12

Preheat the oven to 190°C (375°F) Gas 5.

Whisk together the buttermilk, melted butter and egg in a large jug/pitcher. Sift together the flour, cocoa and raising agents in a separate large mixing bowl and add the sugar and salt. Pour the dry ingredients into the wet and use a fork to gently combine. Do not over mix the batter. Fold in 100 g/⅔ cup of the chocolate chips.

Pour the batter into the paper cases, sprinkle over the remaining chocolate chips and bake in the preheated oven for 20–25 minutes, or until an inserted skewer comes out clean.

Transfer the muffins onto a wire rack to cool slightly before tucking in.

chocolate scones

Teatime wouldn't be complete without a plate of freshly baked scones with clotted cream and jam. I have upped the afternoon ante with a light sifting of cocoa powder to add a little extra indulgence to this classic British staple.

240 g/2 cups self-raising/ rising flour, plus extra for dusting
25 g/2½ tablespoons cocoa powder
1 teaspoon baking powder
a pinch of salt
75 g/5 tablespoons butter, cut into cubes
75 g/⅔ cup caster/ granulated sugar
160 ml/⅔ cup milk
2 teaspoons freshly squeezed lemon juice
1 egg, beaten

To serve

clotted cream
strawberry or raspberry jam/jelly

a 5-cm/2-in. round cookie cutter

Makes 8–10

Preheat the oven to 220°C (425°F) Gas 7 and set a large baking sheet inside the oven to heat.

Sift the flour, cocoa, baking powder and salt into a large mixing bowl. Add the butter and rub it in with your fingers, until the mixture resembles fine breadcrumbs. Stir in the sugar and make a well in the centre. Stir the lemon juice into the milk in a separate jug/pitcher, then add the liquid to the dry ingredients. Combine it quickly using a butter knife – this will help to prevent over-handling the dough, which will make your scones tough.

Tip the dough out onto a lightly floured surface. Scatter a little extra flour over the dough and on your hands and lightly knead the dough. Roll or pat the dough down to make a 4-cm/1½-in. deep round.

Dip the cookie cutter into some flour, then plunge it into the dough – do not twist the cutter as this can affect the rise. Repeat until you can make no more scones and squidge the dough back together before patting down and cutting out some more. Brush the tops with a little beaten egg.

Carefully remove the hot baking sheet from the oven and arrange the scones on it. Bake in the preheated oven for 10–12 minutes, or until well risen. Scones are best eaten on the day, still warm and generously smothered with clotted cream and strawberry or raspberry jam/jelly.

chocolate and beetroot mini loaf cakes

200 g/1 cup light muscovado/brown sugar

100 ml/⅓ cup plus 1 tablespoon sunflower oil

3 large eggs

1 teaspoon vanilla paste

225 g/1 lb. peeled and cooked beetroot/beets (approx. 2–3 beetroot/ beets), blended to a purée

200 g/6½ oz. dark/ bittersweet chocolate (60–70% cocoa solids), melted and cooled

50 g/⅓ cup ground almonds

115 g/1 scant cup self-raising/rising flour

½ teaspoon bicarbonate of/baking soda

½ teaspoon baking powder

a pinch of salt

Icing

50 g/1½ oz. dark/ bittersweet chocolate (60–70% cocoa solids), chopped

25 g/2 tablespoons butter

40 ml/2½ tablespoons sweetened condensed milk

2 tablespoons golden/light corn syrup

Chocolate and courgette/zucchini loaf variation

250 g/8 oz. courgettes/ zucchini, coarsely grated

1 teaspoon ground cinnamon (optional)

12 mini loaf moulds (each 8 x 4 cm/3¼ x 1¾ in.), greased and set on a baking sheet (or a 900-g/ 2-lb. loaf pan, greased – see Note)

Makes 12

Beets adds a mild note of earthiness that makes these cakes incredibly moist. The courgette/zucchini also adds moisture, while a hint of spice enlivens the chocolate.

Preheat the oven to 180°C (350°F) Gas 4.

Put the sugar, oil, eggs and vanilla in a large mixing bowl and whisk until frothy. Add the puréed beetroot/beet, melted chocolate and ground almonds and whisk again until fully mixed. Sift the flour and raising agents, and add the salt before folding in.

Pour the batter into the mini loaf moulds and bake in the preheated oven for 20–25 minutes, or until an inserted skewer comes out clean.

Transfer the loaves, still in their moulds, to a wire rack to cool completely.

To make the icing, simply melt and stir all the ingredients together in a heatproof bowl suspended over a pan of barely simmering water until smooth and glossy. Drizzle the icing over the top of the cakes and enjoy.

Chocolate and courgette/zucchini loaf

You can substitute courgettes/zucchini for the beetroots/beets in these mini vegetable loaf cakes, simply add where you would the beetroots/beets as above along with the ground cinnamon to balance the flavours.

Note

If using a 900-g/2-lb. loaf pan, simply adjust the baking time to 45 minutes–1 hour, or until an inserted skewer comes out clean.

large cakes

Chocolate cakes are ideal for
sharing on a special occasion
– tortes, rings and layer cakes
are show-stoppers!

kladdkaka

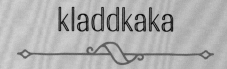

This Swedish chocolate mud cake has a sticky, gooey centre and is delicious served with whipped cream.

2 eggs

300 g/1½ cups caster/
  granulated sugar

65 g/½ cup plain/
  all-purpose flour

40 g/⅓ cup cocoa powder

a pinch of salt

2 teaspoons vanilla extract

1 tablespoon dark rum

115 g/1 stick butter, melted

ice cream or whipped
  cream, to serve

a 20-cm/8-in. round pie
  plate, greased

Serves 6–8

Preheat the oven to 150°C (300°F) Gas 2.

Crack the eggs into a mixing bowl and add the sugar. Sift in the dry ingredients and whisk. Add the vanilla, rum and melted butter and whisk to combine.

Pour the batter into the prepared pie plate and bake in the preheated oven for 30–35 minutes. The cake will still be very gooey in the middle. Serve hot with ice cream or leave to cool and serve with whipped cream.

black forest pavlova

Pavlova was created in the 1920s in honour of ballet dancer Anna Pavlova. Either an Australian or New Zealand invention – neither side can agree – I've added Germany into the equation, giving it the Black Forest treatment.

6 egg whites

a pinch of salt

335 g/1²/₃ cups caster/ superfine sugar

1 teaspoon white wine vinegar

75 g/3½ oz. dark/ bittersweet chocolate (60–70% cocoa solids), grated

20 g/2½ tablespoons cocoa powder, sifted

600 ml/2½ cups double/whipping cream

Kirsch-soaked cherries

600 g/4 cups stoned/pitted cherries

3 tablespoons caster/ granulated sugar

5–6 tablespoons kirsch (or other cherry liqueur)

a large baking sheet lined with baking parchment

Serves 8

Preheat the oven to 150°C (300°F) Gas 2.

Whisk the egg whites with the salt until stiff peaks form. Gradually, 1 tablespoon at a time, add the sugar, whisking between each addition. The meringue should be very stiff and glossy. Whisk in the cocoa and vinegar and fold in the chocolate with a large metal spoon.

Spoon generous dollops of meringue in a ring shape about 25 cm/10 in. across onto the prepared baking sheet. Spoon more of the mixture in the middle and build up the sides slightly higher. Make swirls in the meringue using a fork for an attractive finish. Pop the meringue in the preheated oven, close the oven door and immediately reduce the temperature to 140°C (275°F) Gas 1. Bake for 1 hour.

Turn the oven off, but leave the meringue inside, with the oven door shut, until the oven is completely cold. It's easiest to make the meringue in the evening and leave it in the oven overnight to cool.

For the kirsch-soaked cherries, put the cherries in a bowl and sprinkle the sugar over the top. Pour in the kirsch and toss until all the cherries are completely coated. Cover the bowl with clingfilm/plastic wrap and leave to macerate for a few hours or even overnight while the meringue is also cooling.

Whip the cream until stiff but not dry and whisk in 3–4 tablespoons of the macerating liquor from the cherries. Place the meringue on a cake stand and spread the cream thickly over the top, before piling on the drained cherries.

6 large eggs, separated
a pinch of salt
175 g/³/4 cup plus
   2 tablespoons caster/
   granulated sugar
200 g/6½ oz. dark/
   bittersweet chocolate
   (60–70% cocoa solids),
   melted and cooled slightly
40 g/⅓ cup chestnut flour
icing/confectioners' sugar,
   to dust

Meringue mushrooms

1 egg white
a pinch of salt
50 g/⅓ cup caster/
   superfine sugar
50 g/1½ oz. dark/
   bittersweet chocolate
   (60–70% cocoa solids),
   melted and cooled

Ganache

300 g/10 oz. dark/
   bittersweet chocolate,
   chopped
300 ml/1¼ cups double/
   heavy cream

Chestnut filling

250 g/8 oz. sweetened
   chestnut purée
100 g/6½ tablespoons soft
   butter
1 teaspoon vanilla paste
350 g/3 cups icing/
   confectioners' sugar

a piping/pastry bag fitted
   with a plain nozzle/tip
1–2 baking sheets lined with
   baking parchment or
   silicone paper
a 23 x 32-cm/9 x 13-in.
   swiss roll/jellyroll pan
   lined with baking
   parchment

Serves 8–10

chocolate and chestnut bûche de noël

You can have Christmas all wrapped up with this festive gluten-free chestnut-flavoured Yule log.

Preheat the oven to 100°C (220°F) Gas ¼.

First, make the meringue mushrooms. Whisk the egg white with the salt until stiff, before gradually adding the sugar, a little at a time, whisking between each addition. Spoon the mixture into the piping/pastry bag and pipe little rounds of about 5-cm/2-in. wide onto one of the prepared baking sheets. Next, pipe little upright peaks for the mushroom stalks. Bake in the preheated oven for 1 hour, turn off the oven and leave to cool and dry out, preferably overnight. Once cool, paint the underside of each cap with melted chocolate, glue the stalks onto the caps with a little more melted chocolate. Leave to set.

Preheat the oven to 180°C (350°F) Gas 4.

Whisk the egg whites and salt until stiff. In a separate bowl, whisk the yolks and caster/granulated sugar until pale, thick and creamy. Whisk the chocolate and chestnut flour into the sugar and yolks before vigorously beating in a couple of tablespoons of whisked egg whites to slacken the mixture. Gently fold in the remaining whites with a large metal spoon. Pour the batter into the prepared pan and bake in the preheated oven for about 20 minutes, or until an inserted skewer comes out clean. While still warm, upturn the cake onto a fresh piece of baking parchment with a clean kitchen cloth laid underneath. Peel off the baking parchment and carefully roll the cake up, using the kitchen cloth to help.

To make the ganache, simply heat the cream to just boiling point in a saucepan set over a gentle heat. Pour the hot cream over the chocolate in a heatproof bowl and mix with a spatula until smooth, thick and glossy. Leave to cool.

To make the chestnut filling, simply whisk the chestnut purée, butter and vanilla together before sifting in half of the icing/confectioners' sugar. Once combined, sift in the remaining icing/confectioners' sugar and whisk until light and fluffy.

Unroll the cold cake and spread the chestnut filling evenly over the top. Roll the cake up again and place on a serving board. Spread with a generous coating of ganache using a palette knife and scratch and scrape the surface using a knife or fork to make it look like tree bark. Leave to cool at room temperature until completely set. Dust with icing/confectioners' sugar and arrange the meringue mushrooms in clusters on and around the cake.

prinzregententorte

This Bavarian torte was created in honour of the Prince Regent Luitpold who became Prince Regent in 1866.

8 eggs, separated
a pinch of salt
140 g/3/4 cup caster/ superfine sugar
2 teaspoons vanilla paste
140 g/1 cup plus 1 tablespoon plain/ all-purpose flour
1 teaspoon bicarbonate of/ baking soda
50 g/3 tablespoons butter, melted

Rum syrup

100 g/1/2 cup caster/ granulated sugar
3 tablespoons dark rum

Buttercream

250 g/2 sticks soft butter
250 g/8 oz. dark/ bittersweet chocolate (60–70% cocoa solids), melted and cooled
350 g/3 1/4 cups icing/ confectioners' sugar
3–4 tablespoons dark rum

Ganache

150 g/5 oz. dark/ bittersweet chocolate (60–70% cocoa solids), chopped
150 ml/2/3 cup double/ heavy cream

8 sheets of baking parchment, each trimmed to 20 cm/8 in. circles and arranged on baking sheets

Serves 8–10

Preheat the oven to 190°C (375°F) Gas 5.

Whisk the egg whites with salt until stiff. Gradually whisk in half of the sugar to make meringue. In a separate bowl, whisk the egg yolks with the remaining sugar and vanilla until pale, thick and mousse-like. Fold the egg white and yolk mixture together using a large metal spoon. Sift in the flour and bicarbonate of/baking soda and fold again, being careful not to knock the air out of the mixture. Finally, pour the melted butter down the side of the bowl and fold in.

Spoon eight equal amounts of batter on each sheet of parchment and use a palette knife to spread it thinly and neatly up to the edge of each circle. Bake the layers in batches in the preheated oven for 6–8 minutes, or until golden. Cool on top of wire racks, then peel off the parchment and cool completely.

For the rum syrup, simply stir the sugar and 100 ml/scant 1/2 cup of water together in a pan set over a gentle heat until all the sugar has melted. Bring to the boil, then simmer for 1 minute. Turn off the heat and stir in the rum.

To make the buttercream, whisk the butter until very soft, then whisk in the melted chocolate. Sift in half of the icing/confectioners' sugar and whisk until fully incorporated. Repeat with the remaining icing/confectioners' sugar. Add the rum and continue to whisk until the buttercream is very fluffy.

Place one cake layer of sponge on a cake board, brush the top with rum syrup and spread over a thin layer of buttercream. Stack another layer on top, and continue building up the layers until you reach the last circle of sponge cake layer. Do not brush the top with syrup or spread with buttercream. Use a clean baking sheet to press down firmly so the top of your cake is level. Chill the cake in the freezer for 15–20 minutes, then use a long, serrated knife to trim the cake so the sides are neat. Brush the final layer with rum syrup before spreading the remaining buttercream on the top and sides of the cake using a palette knife. Pop the cake in the fridge to chill.

To make the ganache, follow the instructions on page 65, but using the quantities here. Leave to cool until thick enough to pour without the chocolate just running off the sides of the cake. Spoon the ganache on top of the cake and use a palette knife to tease it over the sides of the cake. Set at room temperature before transferring the cake to a serving plate/stand.

chocolate and passion fruit roulade

Passion fruit beautifully cuts through the bitterness and richness of chocolate with a vibrant tang. Swap the passion fruit for Irish Cream for a wintry alternative.

6 large eggs, separated
a pinch of salt
175 g/³/4 cup plus
   2 tablespoons caster/
   granulated sugar
150 g/5 oz. dark/
   bittersweet chocolate
   (60–70% cocoa solids),
   melted and cooled
15 g/2 tablespoons cocoa
   powder

Filling

300 ml/1¼ cups double/
   heavy cream
1 heaped tablespoon icing/
   confectioners' sugar, plus
   extra for dusting
4–6 passion fruits

Irish cream roulade variation

250 ml/1 cup double/heavy
   cream
75 ml/¹/3 cup Baileys® Irish
   cream (or other whiskey
   and cream-based liqueur)

a 23 x 33-cm/9 x 13-in.
   roulade pan lined with
   baking parchment

Serves 10

Preheat the oven to 180°C (350°F) Gas 4.

Whisk the egg whites and salt together until stiff but not dry and set aside. In a separate bowl, whisk the egg yolks and sugar together until pale, thick and mousse-like. Continue to whisk on low speed, while pouring the chocolate down the side of the bowl. Add a couple of spoonfuls of the egg whites and whisk vigorously to slacken the mixture slightly. Use a large metal spoon to fold the egg whites in, using a slicing action. Sift in the cocoa and fold until streak-free. Spoon the mixture into the prepared pan and gently level with a palette knife. Bake in the preheated oven for about 20 minutes, or until an inserted skewer comes out clean.

Upturn the cake onto a fresh piece of baking parchment while still warm with a clean kitchen cloth positioned underneath. Peel off the baking parchment from the base and carefully roll the cake up, using the kitchen cloth. Set aside to cool.

To make the filling, simply whip the cream until stiff but not dry, sift in the icing/confectioners' sugar and fold.

Unroll the cold cake and spread the cream evenly over the top, leaving a small gap around the edges. Scoop out the passion fruit flesh and seeds and layer on top of the cream. Roll the cake up again, sift over some icing/confectioners' sugar and transfer (seam side down) onto a serving plate.

Irish cream roulade

For a rich alternative, replace the filling above with a mixture of whipped cream and Baileys® Irish cream.

banana and chocolate battenberg

Battenberg is thought to be named in honour of Princess Victoria's marriage to Prince Louis of Battenberg in 1884.

Banana cake

85 g/scant ½ cup caster/
  granulated sugar
85 g/6 tablespoons butter
1 large egg
25 g/2½ tablespoons
  ground almonds
60 g/½ cup self-raising/
  rising flour, sifted
½ teaspoon baking powder
a small pinch of salt
1 teaspoon vanilla extract
1 over-ripe banana, mashed

Chocolate cake

50 g/scant ½ cup self-
  raising/rising flour, sifted
10 g/4 teaspoons cocoa
  powder, sifted

Chocolate marzipan

1 egg
165 g/1 cup plus
  1 tablespoon icing/
  confectioners' sugar
25 g/¼ cup cocoa powder
1 teaspoon lemon juice
1 teaspoon brandy
250 g/2½ cups ground
  almonds

To assemble

100 g/½ cup apricot
  jam/jelly
1 tablespoon cocoa powder

*a 20-cm/8-in. cake pan,
  greased and lined with
  baking parchment*

Serves 8–10

Preheat the oven to 180°C (350°F) Gas 4.

Take a 80-cm/32-in. piece of foil and fold it in half to make it double strength. Measure 10 cm/4 in. from the left and fold the foil. Create a 10-cm/4-in. pleat by folding the foil back towards your left hand and then back towards your right hand. Trim the foil so that it is 20-cm/8-in. wide. Grease the foil and fit it snugly in the cake pan. You should be left with two 10-cm/4-in. compartments.

For the banana cake, put all the ingredients in a large mixing bowl and whisk together for a couple of minutes, or until smooth and creamy. Spoon the batter into one of the foil compartments in the prepared pan. Repeat for the chocolate cake, replacing the quantity of flour and substituting cocoa for the vanilla and banana, then spoon the batter into the other compartment. Level the tops of each half of the cake batter with a clean palette knife.

Bake in the preheated oven for 20–25 minutes, or until an inserted skewer comes out clean. Leave the cakes to cool in the pan for 10 minutes before turning them out onto a wire rack to cool completely.

For the chocolate marzipan, put the egg and sugar in a large heatproof bowl set over a pan of barely simmering water. Whisk continuously until the mixture is pale, thick and has doubled in volume. Keep the heat low or the mixture will curdle. Whisk in the lemon juice and brandy, then take the bowl off the heat and set aside. When cool, pour in the ground almonds and sift in the cocoa, stir to combine, then knead to form a firm dough. Wrap in clingfilm/plastic wrap and rest somewhere cool for at least 2 hours before rolling out.

To assemble, trim each sponge cake to the same size and cut in half lengthways. Warm the jam/jelly in a saucepan set over a gentle heat and push it through a fine mesh sieve/strainer. Brush some jam/jelly along one side of a thin rectangle of banana cake and stick a rectangle of the chocolate cake next to it. Repeat with the other rectangles of chocolate and banana cake to create a checkerboard effect. Roll out the marzipan on a surface lightly dusted with cocoa and trim it to a rectangle of 40 x 23 cm/16 x 9 in., with the shortest side facing towards you. Brush the marzipan with more jam/jelly and stick the cake to the edge of the marzipan closest to you. Carefully roll up until the cake is entirely encased in marzipan. Press the edges of the marzipan together and turn it over so that the join is at the base of the cake. Trim off the excess marzipan at the ends to create a neat finish.

honeycomb cake

Crunchy homemade honeycomb and rich, fluffy chocolate sponge makes this cake a hit with the whole family.

100 g/3½ oz. dark/
  bittersweet chocolate,
  broken into pieces
75 g/⅓ cup dark
  muscovado/brown sugar
200 ml/¾ cup milk
150 g/¾ cup light
  muscovado/brown sugar
75 g/5 tablespoons butter
2 large eggs, beaten
1 teaspoon vanilla extract
a pinch of salt
25 g/3½ tablespoons cocoa
  powder
125 g/1 cup plain/
  all-purpose flour
1 teaspoon bicarbonate of/
  baking soda

Honeycomb

100 g/scant ½ cup light
  runny honey
140 g/½ cup plus
  1 tablespoon liquid glucose
  (or light corn syrup)
100 g/½ cup caster/
  granulated sugar
50 g/¼ cup light
  muscovado/brown sugar
2½ teaspoons bicarbonate
  of/baking soda

Chocolate buttercream

100 g/6½ tablespoons soft
  butter
175 g/1½ cups icing/
  confectioners' sugar
100 g/3½ oz. dark/
  bittersweet chocolate,
  melted and cooled
a splash of milk, if needed

*a baking sheet lined with
  baking parchment*
*2 x 20-cm/8-in. cake pans,
  greased and lined with
  baking parchment*

Serves 8

Preheat the oven to 180°C (350°F) Gas 4.

First, make the honeycomb. Put the honey, glucose, sugars and 50 ml/ 3 tablespoons of water into a large, heavy-based saucepan and stir over a gentle heat until the sugar has fully dissolved. Increase the heat and boil until it reaches the hard-crack stage – 150°C (300°F) on a sugar thermometer – it will be golden around the edges of the pan and if you drop a tiny bit of syrup in a glass of cold water it should immediately solidify into a ball. Quickly stir in the bicarbonate of/baking soda – be very careful, as it will immediately erupt into a frothing, foaming mass. Ensuring you tip the honeycomb away from you as you do it, pour the mixture onto the prepared baking sheet. Carefully tip the sheet back and forth to even it out but don't spread it with a palette knife or you'll lose the bubbly crunchiness. Leave to cool for at least an hour, before peeling it off the baking parchment.

To make the cake, put the chocolate, the dark muscovado/brown sugar and milk in a saucepan set over a gentle heat. Stir until the chocolate and sugar have melted and leave the mixture to cool. Whisk the remaining sugar with the butter until pale and creamy. Gradually beat in the egg before adding the vanilla, salt and whisking in the cooled chocolate milk. Sift the dry ingredients over the liquid and fold in. Divide the batter between the prepared cake pans and bake in the preheated oven for 20–25 minutes, or until an inserted skewer comes out clean. Leave the cakes to cool in their pans on top of a wire rack for 10 minutes before turning out to cool completely.

To make the buttercream, whisk the butter for a few seconds until pale and creamy, before sifting in half of the icing/confectioners' sugar and whisking again until everything is combined. Add the chocolate and whisk through before sifting in the remaining icing/confectioners' sugar. Whisk for a few minutes, adding a splash of milk to slightly slacken the buttercream if you need to. Smash the honeycomb into pieces with a rolling pin, keeping about half of it in chunky pieces for the top of the cake and smash the rest in a sandwich bag into a powder (don't worry if it starts sticking together a bit). Whisk the honeycomb powder into the buttercream.

Sandwich the cakes together with half of the buttercream and spread the remaining half over the top of the cake. Pile the remaining honeycomb on top of the cake just before serving

white chocolate and earl grey cake

Why settle for a cup of tea with your cake, when you can have a cup of tea in your cake? Fluffy and fragrant, this cake is perfect for any celebration.

3 tablespoons Earl Grey loose tea leaves
200 ml/³/₄ cup milk
3 duck eggs (or 4 hen's eggs), separated
a pinch of salt
175 g/1¹/₂ sticks butter
200 g/1 cup caster/granulated sugar
1 teaspoon vanilla paste
150 g/5 oz. white chocolate, melted and cooled
300 g/2¹/₃ cups self-raising/rising flour
edible gold leaf

White chocolate buttercream

2 tablespoons Earl Grey loose tea leaves
200 g/1 stick plus 6 tablespoons soft butter
200 g/7 oz. white chocolate, melted and cooled
350 g/2¹/₂ cups icing/confectioners' sugar
1 teaspoon vanilla paste

2 x 20-cm/8-in. cake pans, greased and lined with baking parchment

Serves 8

Preheat the oven to 180°C (350°F) Gas 4.

Put the tea and milk in a saucepan and slowly bring to the boil over a gentle heat. Once boiling, turn off the heat and leave to cool. Strain the cold, infused milk with a fine mesh sieve/strainer over a jug/pitcher and discard the tea.

Whisk the egg whites and salt until stiff, but not dry. Set aside. In a different bowl, but using the same whisk (no need to wash them up in between), cream the butter and sugar until pale and creamy. Gradually add the egg yolks, one at a time. Whisk in the vanilla, tea-infused milk and white chocolate. Sift in the flour and fold the white chocolate mixture. Next, fold in the beaten egg whites until fully incorporated. Be careful not to knock the air out of the batter.

Divide the mixture between the prepared cake pans and bake in the preheated oven for 20–25 minutes, or until an inserted skewer comes out clean. Leave the cakes to cool in their pans on top of a wire rack for 10 minutes, before turning out and leaving to cool completely.

To make the buttercream, leave the tea to infuse in 3 tablespoons of boiling water for 5 minutes. Strain and discard the tea leaves. Leave the tea to get cold.

Whisk the butter until very soft. Add the chocolate and whisk in. Sift in half of the icing/confectioners' sugar and whisk until combined and creamy. Sift in the remaining icing/confectioners' sugar and whisk to combine before adding the cold tea and vanilla, and whisking until very soft and creamy.

Sandwich the cakes together with one-third of the buttercream and spread the remaining buttercream over the top and sides of the cake with a palette knife. Decorate the top with gold leaf and serve.

chocolate and pink peppercorn torte

Sophisticated and close-textured, this is a cake for grown-ups. Whether you choose to keep it classic with a torte caprese or add a little warming heat with pink peppercorns, you'll find it hard to resist a second slice.

250 g/8 oz. dark/
bittersweet chocolate
(60–70% cocoa solids),
chopped
250 g/2 sticks butter
6 large eggs, separated
a pinch of salt
125 g/²⁄₃ cup caster/
granulated sugar
100 g/²⁄₃ cup ground
almonds
1 tablespoon ground pink
peppercorns
a handful or two of whole
pink peppercorns, to
decorate

Ganache

150 g/5 oz. dark/
bittersweet chocolate
(60–70% cocoa solids),
chopped
150 ml/²⁄₃ cup double/
heavy cream

Torte caprese variation

1 teaspoon vanilla extract
icing/confectioners' sugar,
to dust

*a 23-cm/9-in. cake pan,
greased and lined with
baking parchment*

Serves 8

Preheat 170°C (325°F) Gas 3.

Melt the chocolate and butter together in a heatproof bowl suspended over a pan of barely simmering water. Take the bowl off the heat and cool slightly.

Whisk the egg whites with a pinch of salt until stiff, but not dry and set aside. In a separate bowl, but with the same beaters (there's no need to wash them up in between), whisk the egg yolks and sugar until pale, thick and mousse-like.

Pour the melted chocolate and butter down the side of the bowl gradually, while continuing to whisk. Once streak free, add the ground almonds, ground pink peppercorns and a large spoonful of the beaten egg whites and fold in. Be careful not to knock the air out of the mixture. Lastly, fold the remaining egg whites into the cake batter with a large metal spoon, using a slicing action to ensure you can keep as much air in the batter as possible.

Spoon the mixture into the prepared cake pan, gently level the top with a palette knife and bake in the preheated oven for 30–40 minutes. The cake will continue to cook on cooling, so don't be worried if an inserted cake skewer comes out a bit sticky. You want this cake to have a moist and truffly centre. Leave the cake to cool entirely in its pan, before turning out on a wire rack with a sheet of baking parchment underneath.

To make the ganache, put the chopped chocolate in a heatproof bowl. Heat the cream in a saucepan until it just boils and pour it over the chocolate. Leave for 1 minute before stirring in with a rubber spatula until the chocolate has completely melted and you have a thick, glossy ganache. Leave to cool a little, before pouring over the cake, teasing to the edges and over the sides of the cake with a palette knife – the baking parchment will catch any drips to prevent a big mess on your worktop.

Scatter the pink peppercorns over the top and leave to set at room temperature.

Torte caprese

Transform this peppercorn torte into a classic torte caprese by replacing the ground and whole pink peppercorns with vanilla and leaving out the ganache.

mulled wine chocolate wreath

This port-spiked chocolate cake is pure luxury.
With subtle spicing and notes of orange, this Bundt makes
the ideal last minute Christmas centrepiece to impress
friends and family.

375 ml/1²/₃ cups port
3 large eggs
350 ml/1½ cups milk
185 g/1½ sticks butter,
   melted and cooled
400 g/2 cups caster/
   granulated sugar
grated zest and freshly
   squeezed juice of 1 orange
1 teaspoon vanilla paste
a generous pinch of salt
335 g/2²/₃ cups plain/
   all-purpose flour
125 g/1 cup cocoa powder
2 teaspoons baking powder
2 teaspoons bicarbonate of/
   baking soda
¼ teaspoon ground cloves
1 tablespoon ground
   cinnamon
¼ teaspoon ground nutmeg
winter fruits, to decorate

Glaze

75 g/2½ oz. dark/
   bittersweet chocolate,
   broken into pieces
75 g/5 tablespoons butter,
   cut into cubes
1 tablespoon golden/light
   corn syrup
50 ml/3 tablespoons port

a 25-cm/10-in. cake ring/
   Bundt pan, greased and
   floured

Serves 8

Preheat the oven to 180°C (350°F) Gas 4.

Heat the port in a saucepan set over a gentle heat until just boiling. In the meantime, whisk together the eggs, milk and melted butter in a large mixing bowl. Mix in the sugar, orange zest and juice, vanilla and salt. Sift in the flour, cocoa and raising agents and add the spices before whisking until thoroughly combined. Continue to whisk while gradually adding the hot port. The batter will be very wet.

Pour the mixture into the prepared cake pan and bake in the preheated oven for 40–45 minutes, or until an inserted skewer comes out clean. Leave the cake to cool in its pan on top of a wire rack for 10 minutes, before turning out and leaving to cool completely.

Put all of the glaze ingredients into a small pan set over a gentle heat and stir until the chocolate and butter have melted and the glaze is streak free. Leave to cool until thick enough to pour without it rolling off the sides of the cake.

Place a sheet of baking parchment underneath the wire rack to catch any drips. Pour the glaze over the cold cake. Decorate with winter fruits and leave the cake to set completely at room temperature before transferring to a serving plate or cake stand.

white chocolate, pistachio and rose ring

Fresh and summery, this pretty ring cake is aromatic and full of class. It makes an impressive centrepiece and has the added bonus of being extremely simple to make.

250 g/2 sticks soft butter

200 g/1 cup caster/ granulated sugar

5 eggs

2 teaspoons rose water

100 g/3½ oz. white chocolate, melted and cooled

200 g/1⅓ cups ground pistachios

175 g/1⅔ cups plus 1 tablespoon self-raising/ rising flour

1 teaspoon baking powder

a pinch of salt

To decorate

75 g/2½ oz. white chocolate, melted and cooled

35 g/¼ cup unsalted shelled pistachios, finely chopped

1–2 tablespoons edible dried rose petals

a 25-cm/10-in. cake ring/ Bundt pan, greased and floured

Serves 8

Preheat the oven to 160°C (325°F) Gas 3.

Cream the butter and sugar together until light and fluffy. Whisk in the eggs, one at a time, followed by the rose water and white chocolate. Fold in the ground pistachios. Sift in the flour and baking powder and add the salt before folding the dry ingredients into the mixture.

Spoon the mixture into the prepared cake pan and bake in the preheated oven for 50–55 minutes, or until an inserted skewer comes out clean. Leave the cake to cool in its pan for 10 minutes on top of a wire rack, before turning out and leaving to cool completely.

Once cold, place the cake on a serving plate and drizzle the white chocolate over the top before sprinkling with the chopped pistachios and rose petals. Leave the chocolate to set at room temperature before serving.

black velvet cake

The Black Velvet cocktail was first created in 1861 by Brooks' Club in London as a tribute to the late Prince Albert. The cocktail, like this cake, mixes Guinness® with Champagne for an intensely dark and moreish cake.

200 g/6½ oz. dark/
   bittersweet chocolate
   (60–70% cocoa solids),
   chopped
225 g/1 stick plus
   7 tablespoons soft butter
350 g/1¾ cups dark
   muscovado/brown sugar
4 large eggs, beaten
440 ml/14 oz. Guinness®
   (or other dry stout)
225 g/1¾ cups plain/
   all-purpose flour
1 teaspoon baking powder
2 teaspoons bicarbonate of/
   baking soda
100 g/¾ cup cocoa powder
a pinch of salt

Frosting

200 g/6½ oz. full-fat cream
   cheese (such as
   Philadelphia)
250 g/2 sticks soft butter
400 g/3½ cups icing/
   confectioners' sugar
2 teaspoons vanilla extract
50 ml/3 tablespoons
   Champagne (or other
   sparkling wine)

*3 x 20-cm/8-in. cake pans,
   greased and lined with
   baking parchment*

Serves 12

Preheat the oven to 180°C (350°F) Gas 4.

Melt the chocolate in a heatproof bowl suspended over a pan of barely simmering water. Leave to cool.

In a separate bowl, cream together the butter and sugar and add the beaten eggs, a little at a time to prevent curdling.

Whisk the Guinness® into the melted chocolate (you might want to decant this into a large jug/pitcher for ease later on).

Sift together the dry ingredients and fold half into the butter and sugar mixture.

Add half of the chocolate mixture and mix thoroughly. Add the remaining dry ingredients, followed by the wet, and whisk until everything is thoroughly mixed.

Spoon the batter into the prepared cake pans and bake in the preheated oven for 20–25 minutes, or until an inserted skewer comes out clean. Leave the cakes to cool on a wire rack still in their pans, before turning out.

To make the frosting, whisk the butter and cream cheese together before sifting in half of the icing/confectioners' sugar. Whisk to combine, before sifting in the remaining icing/confectioners' sugar. Continue to whisk until combined, then add the vanilla and Champagne. Continue to whisk until light and fluffy.

Place one of the cake layers on a serving plate or cake stand. Layer the cakes on top of each other using two-thirds of the frosting, before spreading the remaining third on the top of the cake with a palette knife.

praline opera cake

———————⬤———————

This French cake is pure opulence. I have used hazelnuts and praline paste for an extra touch of glamour.

1 tablespoon caster/granulated sugar dissolved in 150 ml/⅔ cup espresso
50 g/1½ oz. dark/bittersweet chocolate, tempered (see page 31)
150 ml/⅔ cup hazelnut liqueur (I use Frangelico)
gold leaf, to decorate

Hazelnut *Joconde*

2 eggs plus 2 egg yolks and 5 whites
175 g/1½ cups icing/confectioners' sugar, sifted
175 g/1¼ cups ground hazelnuts
40 g/3 tablespoons butter, melted
50 g/⅓ cup plus 1 tablespoon plain/all-purpose flour, sifted
a pinch of salt
50 g/¼ cup caster/superfine sugar

French buttercream

200 g/1 cup caster/granulated sugar
3 egg yolks, whisked
200 g/1 stick plus 5 tablespoons soft butter
2 tablespoons hazelnut liqueur
3 tablespoons praline paste

Ganache

250 g/8 oz. dark/bittersweet chocolate, chopped
250 ml/1 cup single/light cream
25 g/2 tablespoons butter

2 x 38 x 25-cm/15 x 10-in. roulade/jellyroll pans lined with baking parchment

Serves 12–15

Preheat the oven to 180°C (350°F) Gas 4.

First, make the *Joconde*. Whisk the eggs, egg yolks and icing/confectioners' sugar together until pale and fluffy. Add the ground hazelnuts and continue whisking for about 5 minutes. Stir in the melted butter and flour until thoroughly mixed. In a separate, clean and oil-free bowl, whisk the egg whites and salt until stiff, but not dry. Whisk in the caster/superfine sugar in two stages and continue whisking until the meringue is stiff and glossy. Add a third of the meringue to the nut mixture and vigorously stir in to slacken the batter. Fold in the remaining meringue and pour the mixture into the prepared cake pans. Use a palette knife to smooth the mixture out thinly. Bake in the preheated oven for 8–12 minutes, or until the *Joconde* is no longer sticky to touch. Keep a close eye on it, as it can burn very quickly. Remove from the oven and leave to cool in its pan on top of a wire rack for about 10 minutes before turning onto the rack to cool completely.

To make the French buttercream, put the sugar and 2 tablespoons of water in a pan set over a gentle heat and stir until the sugar has dissolved. Increase the heat slightly and simmer until it reaches the soft ball stage – this happens at around 113°C (235°F). Put the whisked egg yolks in a large mixing bowl and trickle the hot syrup in, whisking all the time. Once pale and fluffy, leave the mixture to cool a little before whisking in the butter. Whisk in the liqueur and leave to cool completely. Fold in the praline and set aside until ready to use.

Make the chocolate ganache following the instructions on page 65 but using the quantities here, whisking in the butter at the end before cooling.

To assemble, trim both the sheets of *Joconde* into rectangles, cut each rectangle in half so that you have 4 pieces of cake. Turn one piece of *Joconde* over and paint it with the tempered chocolate to make a crisp chocolate base. Set at room temperature before turning it over. Apply a liberal amount of the sweet espresso to the top to turn the cake brown. Evenly spread a layer of buttercream about 5 mm/¼ in. thick over the espresso-soaked sponge and place another layer of *Joconde* on top. Soak the cake in hazelnut liqueur this time. Spread a thin, even layer of ganache over the top. Leave to set at room temperature. Top with a third layer of *Joconde* and soak with more sweet espresso. Spread with another layer of buttercream before placing the final layer of *Joconde* on top. Soak in hazelnut liqueur and top with more ganache. Set at room temperature. Decorate with a little gold leaf for extra glamour, trim the edges and serve.

chocolate and cola cake

Moist and rich, but in no way sickly, this chocolate and cola cake makes the perfect child's birthday cake.

2 large eggs, beaten
250 ml/1 cup milk
125 ml/1 cup sunflower oil
1 teaspoon vanilla paste
250 ml/1 cup flat cola
225 g/1¾ cups plain/
    all-purpose flour
250 g/1¼ cups caster/
    granulated sugar
85 g/⅔ cup cocoa powder
1½ teaspoons baking
    powder
1½ teaspoons bicarbonate
    of/baking soda
a pinch of salt
cola bottle sweets, to
    decorate (optional)

Chocolate buttercream

150 g/1 stick plus
    2 tablespoons soft butter
250 g/2¼ cups icing/
    confectioners' sugar
150 g/5 oz. dark/
    bittersweet chocolate
    (60–70% cocoa solids),
    melted and cooled
a splash of milk, if needed

2 x 20-cm/8-in. cake pans,
    greased and lined with
    baking parchment

Serves 8

Preheat the oven to 180°C (350°F) Gas 4.

Whisk together the eggs, milk, oil, vanilla and cola in a large jug/pitcher. Sift in the dry ingredients and whisk to combine. This is a very liquid batter.

Divide the mixture between the prepared cake pans and bake in the preheated oven for 25–30 minutes, or until an inserted skewer comes out clean. Leave the cakes to cool in their pans on a wire rack for 10 minutes, before turning out and leaving to cool completely.

To make the buttercream, whisk the butter for a few seconds until pale and creamy, before sifting in half of the icing/confectioners' sugar and whisking again until everything is combined. Add the chocolate and whisk through before sifting in the remaining icing/confectioners' sugar. Whisk for a few minutes, adding a splash of milk to slightly slacken the mixture if you need to.

Sandwich the cakes together with just under half of the buttercream and use a palette knife to spread the remaining buttercream on the top and sides of the cake. Scatter over a handful or so of cola bottles to decorate and serve.

pastries

Irresistibly chocolatey tarts, tartlets, mille feuille, pastries, buns, brioche and more.

chocolate mille feuille

Mille feuilles means 'a thousand leaves' – layers
of buttery chocolate puff filled with crème pâtissière.

icing/confectioners' sugar,
for dusting

Chocolate puff pastry

125 g/1 cup plain/
all-purpose flour
35 g/⅓ cup cocoa powder
a pinch of salt
50–75 ml/¼–⅓ cup cold
water
2 teaspoons freshly
squeezed lemon juice
125 g/1 stick cold butter

Crème pâtissière

200 ml/¾ cup milk
2 large egg yolks
50 g/¼ cup caster/
granulated sugar
20 g/2½ tablespoons
cornflour/cornstarch, sifted
1 teaspoon vanilla paste
15 g/1 tablespoon butter
35 g/1 oz. dark/bittersweet
chocolate (60–70% cocoa
solids), melted and cooled
slightly

*2 piping/pastry bags
fitted with 1-cm/⅜-in.
plain nozzles/tips*
*2 baking sheets lined with
baking parchment*

Makes 8–10

First make the chocolate puff pastry following the instructions on page 108.

Preheat the oven to 190°C (375°F) Gas 5.

Cut the puff pastry in half and roll each piece until it is about 1.5-mm/¹⁄₁₆-in. thick. Prick the tops all over with a fork and arrange one rectangle of pastry on each prepared baking sheet. Place another sheet of baking parchment over the pastry and top each rectangle with another clean baking sheet. Bake in the preheated oven for 15–20 minutes, or until cooked through and dry to the touch. Remove from the oven and turn the heat up to 220°C (450°F) Gas 8. Remove the top baking sheets and peel off the top layer of baking parchment, before liberally dusting with icing/confectioners' sugar. Return the pastry to the oven for a few minutes, or until the sugar has caramelized. Be careful, it can turn very quickly!

Leave the pastry to cool for a few minutes, before trimming the edges and cutting into 10 x 3-cm/4 x 1¼-in. rectangles. Leave to cool completely.

To make the two different flavours of crème pâtissière, start by making a basic vanilla pastry cream. Put the milk in a pan set over a gentle heat. In the meantime, put the egg yolks, sugar, cornflour/cornstarch and vanilla in a heatproof bowl and whisk together. Once the milk just comes to the boil, pour it over the eggs and whisk together. Pour the mixture back into the pan and stir continuously over a gentle heat for 1–2 minutes. Increase the heat and continuing to stir until the mixture has thickened. Take the pan off the heat and vigorously whisk in the butter until it has melted. Spoon half of the crème pâtissière into a bowl and cover with clingfilm/plastic wrap to prevent a skin forming. Whisk the melted chocolate into the remaining half before decanting into another bowl and covering. Leave to cool to room temperature before spooning the mixtures into the piping/pastry bags. Chill until needed.

To assemble the *mille feuilles*, simply pipe rounds of vanilla crème pâtissière onto 10 rectangles. Top with a second rectangle of pastry, before piping them with even rounds of chocolate crème pâtissière. Finally, place a third rectangle of pastry on each, before using a palette knife to transfer the *mille feuilles* to serving plates. Dust with icing/confectioners' sugar and serve.

tarte au chocolat

This chocolate tart is a timeless classic and makes an elegant make-ahead dinner party dessert.

80 g/⅔ cup icing/ confectioners' sugar

180 g/1½ cups plain/ all-purpose flour

100 g/6½ tablespoons cold butter, cut into cubes

1 egg yolk

1 tablespoon cold milk

a pinch of salt

seeds of 1 vanilla pod/bean

1 egg white, beaten, for glazing

Filling

300 g/10 oz. dark/ bittersweet chocolate (60–70% cocoa solids), finely chopped

300 ml/1¼ cups double/ heavy cream

2 level tablespoons light muscovado/brown sugar

a pinch of salt

3 large eggs, beaten

a 23-cm/9-in. loose-bottomed tart pan

Serves 8

To make the pastry, blitz the icing/confectioners' sugar and flour in a food processor until well mixed. Add the butter and pulse until the mixture resembles fine breadcrumbs. Add the egg yolk, milk, salt and vanilla and pulse again until just combined. Tip the soft dough onto a sheet of clingfilm/plastic wrap, wrap it up and pop it in the fridge to rest for an hour.

Take two sheets of clingfilm/plastic wrap and place the pastry between them before rolling it out to about 5-mm/¼-in. thick. Remove the top layer of clingfilm/plastic wrap and transfer the pastry to the prepared tart pan. Gently push the pastry into place with your thumbs. Slice off any overhanging pastry and carefully peel off the clingfilm/plastic wrap. Prick the base with a fork and pop it in the fridge until chilled and firm.

Preheat the oven to 180°C (350°F) Gas 4.

Line the pastry with baking parchment – I find the easiest way to do this is to crumple the parchment roughly before sitting it snugly inside the tart case – and cover with baking beans. Bake in the preheated oven for 20 minutes, carefully remove the baking beans and baking parchment, and brush the pastry with the beaten egg white. Return the pastry case to the oven for 5 minutes, then remove and leave to cool on a wire rack while you make the filling.

Reduce the oven temperature to 140°C (275°F) Gas 1.

Place the chopped chocolate in a heatproof bowl and set aside. Put the cream and sugar in a saucepan set over a gentle heat and stir until the sugar has completely dissolved. Stop stirring and increase the heat slightly until the cream comes to the boil. Tip the hot cream over the chocolate along with the salt and leave to stand for 1 minute. Use a rubber spatula to stir the chocolate and cream together until melted and glossy. Whisk in the beaten eggs until fully combined and pour the chocolate mixture into the pastry case.

Place the tart in the oven, close the door and immediately turn the oven off. Leave the tart to bake for 20 minutes. Remove from the oven and leave to cool completely before transferring to the fridge to set for at least 2 hours. Once set, carefully remove the tart from its pan and transfer to a serving plate. Leave to stand at room temperature for half an hour before serving.

80 g/¾ cup icing/
  confectioners' sugar
180 g/1½ cups plain/
  all-purpose flour
100 g/6½ tablespoons cold
  butter, cut into cubes
1 egg yolk
1 tablespoon cold milk
a pinch of salt
seeds of 1 vanilla pod/bean
1 egg white, beaten, for
  glazing
cocoa powder, for dusting
  (optional)

Custard filling

200 g/7 oz. milk/
  semi-sweet chocolate,
  chopped
9 egg yolks
100 g/½ cup golden caster/
  turbinado sugar
225 ml/scant 1 cup
  double/heavy cream
225 ml/scant 1 cup milk
1 vanilla pod/bean, split
  and seeds scraped out

**White chocolate and
tonka bean custard
tart variation**

100 g/3½ oz. white
  chocolate, chopped
2 teaspoons finely grated
  tonka beans, plus extra
  for dusting

*a 23-cm/9-in. loose-
bottomed tart pan*

Serves 8

milk chocolate custard tart

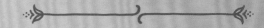

Who can resist a custard tart? Especially one that includes an extra helping of chocolate.

To make the pastry, blitz the icing/confectioners' sugar and flour in a food processor until well mixed. Add the butter and pulse until the mixture resembles fine breadcrumbs. Add the egg yolk, milk, salt and vanilla and pulse again until just combined. Tip the soft dough onto a sheet of clingfilm/plastic wrap, wrap it up and pop it in the fridge to rest for an hour.

Place the pastry between two sheets of clingfilm/plastic wrap before rolling to about 5-mm/¼-in. thick. Remove the top layer of clingfilm/plastic wrap and transfer the pastry to the prepared tart pan. Gently push into place with your thumbs. Slice off any overhanging pastry and carefully peel off the clingfilm/plastic wrap. Prick the base with a fork and chill in the fridge until firm.

Preheat the oven to 180°C (350°F) Gas 4.

Line the pastry with baking parchment – I find the easiest way to do this is to crumple the parchment roughly before sitting it snugly inside the tart case – and cover with baking beans. Bake in the preheated oven for 20 minutes, carefully remove the baking beans and baking parchment, and brush the pastry with the beaten egg white. Return the pastry case to the oven for 5 minutes, then remove and leave to cool on a wire rack. Reduce the heat to 140°C (275°F) Gas 1.

To make the custard, melt the chocolate in a heatproof bowl suspended over a pan of barely simmering water. In the meantime, whisk the egg yolks and sugar until pale and creamy in a heatproof bowl and place a fine mesh sieve/strainer over the top. Put the cream, milk and vanilla in a saucepan and slowly bring to the boil. Pour the hot liquid into the eggs, discarding the vanilla caught by the sieve/strainer. Whisk together, before whisking in the melted chocolate. Pour the chocolate custard into a jug/pitcher and leave to settle for a few minutes before skimming off any froth from the top.

Carefully pour the custard into the pastry case and bake in the preheated oven for 35–40 minutes, or until just set with a slight wobble. Leave to cool completely in the pan on top of a wire rack, then dust with cocoa if you wish.

White chocolate and tonka bean custard tart
For a white chocolate alternative of this tart, simply replace the milk/semi-sweet chocolate with white chocolate and add the tonka beans at the same time. Dust the tart with ground tonka beans instead of cocoa powder to serve.

mascarpone and raspberry tartlets

Fresh and fruity, these dainty tarts are simple to prepare
and make a wonderful end to any meal.

Chocolate pastry

80 g/³/₄ cup icing/
confectioners' sugar
160 g/1¼ cups plain/
all-purpose flour
20 g/1½ tablespoons cocoa
powder
100 g/6½ tablespoons cold
butter, cut into cubes
1 egg yolk
1 tablespoon cold milk
a pinch of salt
1 egg white, beaten, for
glazing

Mascarpone filling

250 g/8 oz. full-fat
mascarpone
300 ml/1¼ cups double/
heavy cream
3 tablespoons icing/
confectioners' sugar, sifted
1 teaspoon vanilla paste

To decorate

750 g/3 pints fresh
raspberries
75 g/3½ oz. dark/
bittersweet chocolate
(60–70% cocoa solids),
chopped

8 x 10-cm/4-in. tart pans

Makes 8

To make the pastry, blitz the icing/confectioners' sugar, flour and cocoa in
a food processor until well mixed. Add the butter and pulse until the mixture
resembles fine breadcrumbs. Add the egg yolk, milk and salt, and pulse again
until just combined. Tip the soft dough onto a sheet of clingfilm/plastic wrap,
wrap it up and pop it in the fridge to rest for an hour.

Cut the pastry into eight equal pieces and roll each out on a lightly floured
surface until the pastry is 3-mm/⅛-in. thick. Line the tart pans, gently pushing the
pastry into place with your thumbs. Slice off any overhanging pastry. Prick the
bases with a fork and chill in the fridge until firm.

Preheat the oven to 180°C (350°F) Gas 4.

Line the pastry with baking parchment – I find the easiest way to do this is to
crumple the parchment roughly before sitting it snugly inside the tart case – and
cover with baking beans. Bake in the preheated oven for 10 minutes, carefully
remove the baking beans and baking parchment, and brush the pastry with the
beaten egg white. Return the pastry case to the oven for 5 minutes, then remove
and leave to cool on a wire rack.

To make the mascarpone filling, simply whisk all the ingredients together until
thick. Divide the filling between the cold pastry cases and level their tops with
a palette knife. Lightly place the raspberries on top of the filling.

Melt the chocolate and leave to cool slightly before drizzling over the tops
of the tarts. Serve immediately or transfer to the fridge until ready to eat.

breakfast pastries

A classic pain au chocolat makes for a heavenly blow-out
breakfast, or why not try chocolate marzipan croissants?

Pain au chocolat

500 g/4 cups white bread
flour
10 g/2 teaspoons salt
50 g/¼ cup caster/
granulated sugar
14 g/4½ teaspoons fast-
acting yeast
350 g/3 sticks butter
240 g/8 oz. dark/
bittersweet chocolate
(60–70% cocoa solids),
chopped

Chocolate marzipan
croissant variation

350 g/12 oz. chocolate
marzipan (recipe page 70),
rolled into 12–14 sausages
1 egg whisked with
2 tablespoons milk
100 g/¾ cup flaked/
slivered almonds
2–3 tablespoons icing/
confectioners' sugar, for
dusting

*a baking sheet lined with
baking parchment*

Makes 12–14

Sift the flour into a large mixing bowl and make a well in the middle. Place the
salt on one side of the bowl and the yeast and sugar on the other. Add 150 ml/
⅔ cup of water and mix together, adding a little extra water (up to 300 ml/
1⅓ cup total), until the mixture forms a dough. Tip the dough out onto a lightly
floured surface and knead for 10 minutes, or until elastic. Put the dough back in
the bowl, cover with clingfilm/plastic wrap and chill in the fridge for 1–3 hours.

Put the butter in between 2 sheets of baking parchment and bash it with a
rolling pin until you have a flat rectangle of butter about 2-cm/¾-in. thick.

On a lightly floured surface, roll the dough into a rectangle, about 1.25-cm/
½-in. thick and place the butter in the centre. Fold the edges of the dough over
the butter to create a neat parcel. Turn the dough over, so the seams are
underneath, and roll into a neat rectangle of about 38 x 20 cm/16 x 8 in. With
a short edge facing you, brush off any excess flour and fold over the furthest
edge towards you and then the edge nearest you over the top. Seal the edges
together with your fingers. Dust the surface with more flour and turn the dough
90 degrees. Roll into a rectangle, brush off any excess flour and fold as before.
Seal the edges with your fingers, wrap the dough in clingfilm/plastic wrap and
rest in the fridge for an hour. Repeat the rolling, folding and resting twice more,
so in the end the dough will have been rolled and folded six times and rested in
the fridge three times. Chill in the fridge for at least 2 hours, the last time.

On a lightly floured work surface, roll the dough out to about 5-mm/¼-in.
thick. Trim the edges and cut the dough into 12 equal squares. Place a row of
chopped chocolate at the bottom of each square. Roll up the dough tightly into
a sausage and place each sausage, seam side down, on the prepared baking
sheet, leaving a good gap between each one. Cover with a clean kitchen cloth
and leave to rise for 2 hours, until doubled in size.

Preheat the oven to 200°C (400°F) Gas 6. Bake for 15–20 minutes, or until
golden and well risen. Cool completely on a wire rack before serving. To enjoy
warm, simply reheat in a warm oven for 5–10 minutes before serving.

Chocolate marzipan croissants
Cut the rolled dough into isosceles triangles. Put a marzipan sausage at the base
of each triangle. Roll up the dough into crescents, brush with egg wash and
scatter over the almonds. Bake as above and dust with icing/confectioners' sugar.

chocolate and passion fruit meringue pies

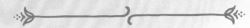

Meringue, chocolate and fragrant, tangy fruits make
a wonderful alternative to the classic lemon.

1 quantity Chocolate pastry
(page 96)

Passion fruit curd

200 g/³⁄₄ cup passion fruit
pulp (about 10–12 fruits'
worth)

150 g/10 tablespoons
butter, cut into cubes

2 eggs plus 2 egg yolks

175 g/³⁄₄ cup plus
2 tablespoons caster/
granulated sugar

1 tablespoon cornflour/
cornstarch

Meringue

4 egg whites

a pinch of salt

200 g/1¹⁄₄ cups caster/
superfine sugar

1¹⁄₂ teaspoons cornflour/
cornstarch

1 teaspoon white wine
vinegar

Lime curd variation

3 tablespoons cornflour/
cornstarch

finely grated zest of 4 limes
and freshly squeezed juice
of 6 limes

100 g/¹⁄₂ cup caster/
granulated sugar

50 g/3 tablespoons butter,
cut into cubes

1 egg and 4 egg yolks

8 x 10-cm/4-in. tart pans

Serves 8

First, make the pastry cases following the instructions on page 96.

To make the passion fruit curd, blitz the pulp in a food processor and pass it all through a fine mesh sieve/strainer. Transfer to a saucepan with the butter and set over a gentle heat. Stir until the butter is melted. Whisk the remaining ingredients together until pale and fluffy. Pour the hot passion fruit mixture into this mixture and whisk together, before pouring it all back into the saucepan. Continue to whisk gently for several minutes until the curd has thickened enough to coat the back of a spoon. Set aside to cool.

To make the meringue, simply whisk the egg whites and salt together until stiff and gradually, one tablespoon at a time, add the sugar, whisking well between each addition. Add the cornflour/cornstarch and vinegar and whisk again.

To assemble the pies, pour the passion fruit curd into the pastry cases and level their tops with a palette knife. Spoon a ring of meringue around the very edge of the filling, to create a seal between the meringue and the pastry, then billow the remaining meringue over the top of each pie and swirl a fork through the top. Bake in the reduced heat oven for 15–20 minutes, or until the meringue is firm and slightly golden. Leave to cool completely in the pans before removing. These pies are best eaten on the day they are made.

Chocolate and lime meringue pies

Replace the passion fruit curd with lime curd for a zesty take on these mini meringue pies. To make the lime curd filling, put the cornflour/cornstarch and 150 ml/²⁄₃ cup of water in a saucepan and stir to form a paste. Add the sugar, lime zest and juice and stir over a medium heat until the mixture has thickened. Take the pan off the heat and whisk in the butter until it has melted. Leave to cool for a couple of minutes. Whisk together the egg and egg yolks, then whisk into the lime mixture. Return the pan to the heat and continue to whisk for 3–4 minutes until the curd has thickened enough to dollop. Assemble the pies as above.

chocolate, pear and frangipane tart

Chocolate-laced frangipane is a difficult indulgence to resist, so why try? Pears or cherries make the perfect match, but you can also try other seasonal fruit, too.

1 quantity Chocolate pastry (page 96)

Poached pears

200 g/1 cup caster/
   granulated sugar
5 long strips of orange peel
freshly squeezed juice of
   1 orange
1 vanilla pod/bean, split
1 cinnamon stick, bruised
4 firm pears, peeled

Chocolate frangipane

125 g/1 stick soft butter
125 g/^{2}/$_3$ cup caster/
   granulated sugar
2 eggs, beaten
seeds of 1 vanilla pod/bean
125 g/1 cup ground
   almonds
3 tablespoons cocoa powder
a pinch of salt

Chocolate and cherry tart variation

250 g/8 oz. stoned/pitted
   and halved cherries

*a 23-cm/9-in. tart pan with
   a removable base*

Serves 8

First, make the chocolate pastry following the instructions on page 96. Roll out the dough between clingfilm/plastic wrap to a thickness of about 3 mm/^{1}/$_8$ in. Remove the top layer of clingfilm/plastic wrap and transfer to the prepared tart pan. Gently push the pastry into place with your thumbs. Slice off any overhanging pastry and carefully peel off the clingfilm/plastic wrap. Prick the base with a fork and chill in the fridge until firm.

Preheat the oven to 180°C (350°F) Gas 4.

Line the pastry with baking parchment and cover with baking beans. Bake for 20 minutes, carefully remove the baking beans and baking parchment, and return the pastry case to the oven for 5–10 minutes, until dry to the touch, then remove and leave to cool on a wire rack.

To poach the pears, put the sugar, 500 ml/2 cups of water, orange peel and juice, vanilla and cinnamon in a saucepan set over a medium heat. Stir every now and then until the sugar has dissolved. Plunge the pears into the poaching syrup and carefully place a large disc of baking parchment on top with a plate on top as a weight. Reduce the heat and simmer for 25 minutes. Remove the pears from the poaching syrup with a slotted spoon and set aside to cool.

Preheat the oven to 190°C (375°F) Gas 5.

To make the chocolate frangipane, cream the butter and sugar together until pale and creamy. Gradually whisk in the eggs, mix in the vanilla and ground almonds before sifting in the cocoa and adding the salt, and folding in. Spread the frangipane evenly in the pastry case.

Slice the pears in half, lengthways, scoop out the core, then cut into thin slices, keeping the shape. Slide one pear half onto a palette knife and press down on the pear slices gently to fan them out. Slide them on top of the frangipane and continue arranging the sliced pears in a circle. Bake in the preheated oven for 1–1 hour and 10 minutes, or until the frangipane has risen and set, and serve.

Chocolate and cherry tart

You could replace the poached pears with cherries, if preferred, and follow the recipe as above.

chocolate and chestnut tart

This wheat-free tart, topped with marron glacés, makes a stylish alternative to Christmas pudding.

6–8 marrons glacés, to decorate

Chocolate chestnut shortcrust pastry

100 g/1 scant cup icing/ confectioners' sugar

100 g/³⁄₄ cup Italian chestnut flour (farina di castagna)

100 g/³⁄₄ cup rice flour

25 g/3¹⁄₂ tablespoons cocoa powder

125 g/1 stick cold butter, cut into cubes

1 large egg yolk

1 tablespoon cold milk

a pinch of salt

1 egg white, beaten, for glazing

Chestnut crème pâtissière

335 ml/2¹⁄₃ cups milk

1 vanilla pod/bean, split with the seeds scraped out

1 whole egg

3 egg yolks

50 g/¹⁄₄ cup caster/ granulated sugar

35 g/¹⁄₃ cup cornflour/ cornstarch, sifted

250 g/8 oz. sweetened chestnut purée

3 tablespoons dark rum

15 g/1 tablespoon butter, cut into small cubes

Ganache

100 g/3¹⁄₂ oz. dark chocolate (60–70% cocoa solids), chopped

100 ml/scant ¹⁄₂ cup double/heavy cream

a 23-cm/9-in. tart pan with a removable base

Serves 8

To make the pastry, blitz the icing/confectioners' sugar, flours and cocoa in a food processor until well mixed. Add the butter and pulse until the mixture resembles fine breadcrumbs. Add the egg yolk, milk, salt and vanilla and pulse again until just combined. Wrap in clingfilm/plastic wrap and chill in the fridge for an hour. Roll out the pastry between clingfilm/plastic wrap to a thickness of about 3 mm/¹⁄₈ in. Remove the top layer of clingfilm/plastic wrap and transfer to the prepared tart pan. Gently push the pastry into place with your thumbs. Slice off any overhanging pastry and carefully peel off the clingfilm/plastic wrap. Prick the base with a fork and chill in the fridge until firm.

Preheat the oven to 180°C (350°F) Gas 4.

Line the pastry with baking parchment and cover with baking beans. Bake for 20 minutes, carefully remove the baking beans and baking parchment, and brush the pastry with the beaten egg white. Return the pastry case to the oven for 5–10 minutes, until dry to the touch, then remove and leave to cool on a wire rack.

To make the chestnut crème pâtissière, put the milk and vanilla in a pan set over a gentle heat and simmer gently for 5 minutes. Put the egg, egg yolks, sugar and cornflour/cornstarch in a heatproof bowl and whisk together. Once the milk just comes to the boil, pour it over the eggs through a fine mesh sieve/strainer and whisk together. Return the mixture to the pan and stir over the heat for 1–2 minutes. Increase the heat and stir until the mixture has thickened. Take the pan off the heat and add the chestnut purée, rum and butter, and whisk vigorously until it has melted. Transfer to a jug/pitcher and cover in clingfilm/ plastic wrap to prevent a skin forming. Once cool, spread the crème pâtissière evenly in the pastry case and chill in the fridge.

To make the ganache, simply place the chocolate and cream in a heatproof bowl and suspend over a pan of barely simmering water and stir with a rubber spatula every now and then, until the chocolate has melted and you have a smooth, glossy ganache. Leave to cool slightly before spreading the ganache evenly over the top of the chestnut crème pâtissière. Leave to set.

Finely chop the marrons glacés and carefully sprinkle them over the top of the tart before serving.

150 ml/²/₃ cup milk or water
75 g/5 tablespoons butter,
   cubed
100 g/³/₄ cup plain/
   all-purpose flour
a pinch of salt
3 large eggs, beaten
225 g/1 pint strawberries,
   hulled and chopped tossed
   in 1 tablespoon caster/
   granulated sugar, to serve

Crème pâtissière

150 ml/²/₃ cup milk
1 egg yolk
25 g/2½ tablespoons
   caster/granulated sugar
20 g/2½ tablespoons
   cornflour/cornstarch
1 teaspoon vanilla paste
15 g/1 tablespoon butter
150 ml/²/₃ cup double/
   heavy cream, whipped

Chocolate glaze

75 g/2½ oz. dark/
   bittersweet chocolate
   (60–70% cocoa solids),
   chopped
1 tablespoon milk
1 tablespoon icing/
   confectioners' sugar, sifted

**Chocolate and
cardamom eclair
variation**

6–8 cardamom pods,
   smashed (optional)

*1 large piping/pastry bag
   fitted with a star nozzle/tip
   and another with a 1-cm/
   ³/₈-in. plain nozzle/tip*
*2 baking sheets lined with
   baking parchment*

Makes 12

strawberry éclairs

◆———————◆———————◆

The word éclair means flash of lightning. These feather-
light pastries are so delicious, they'll be gone in a flash.

First, make the crème pâtissière following the instructions on page 91 but using
the quantities here.

Preheat the oven to 220°C (425°F) Gas 7.

To make the choux/cream puff pastry/paste, put the milk or water in a
saucepan with the butter set over a medium heat. Stir until the butter has melted
and then increase the heat to bring to a rolling boil, before immediately
removing from the heat. Sift in the flour and salt and beat vigorously until the
mixture comes together. Return to a gentle heat, stirring for 1 minute, or until
the mixture starts to come away from the sides of the pan and forms a dough.
Remove from the heat and cool until hand hot. Using a wooden spoon, add a
little of the egg at a time, beating very well in between each addition. You may
not need all the egg; you are aiming for a soft, silky and shiny batter with a
dropping consistency. Spoon the mixture into the other piping/pastry bag and
pipe 12 lines, each about 18-cm/7-in. long, onto the prepared baking sheets.

Bake in the preheated oven for 20 minutes, or until the éclairs have puffed up
and are light golden. Remove from the oven and stab the base of each one with
a skewer to allow the steam to escape. Return to the baking sheets and put back
in the oven for 5 minutes. Turn the oven off, open the door and leave the éclairs
in there for another 5 minutes before transferring to a wire rack to cool.

Once the éclairs are completely cold, make a slit in the side of each éclair and
pipe a generous swirl of crème pâtissière in each one. Top with a good spoonful
of macerated strawberries.

To make the chocolate glaze, simply put all the ingredients in a heatproof bowl
suspended above a pan of barely simmering water and stir until melted and
glossy. Cool slightly before spreading over the tops of the éclairs.

Chocolate and cardamom éclairs

For an indulgent take on these fruity éclairs, make the crème pâtissière, omitting
the vanilla. Instead, add the smashed cardamom pods to the milk, bring to the
boil and leave to infuse until cold before discarding the pods. Fill the éclairs
with the cardamom-flavoured crème pâtissière, omitting the macerated
strawberries and top with chocolate glaze.

chocolate and banana tarte tatin

Homemade chocolate puff pastry is quite a lengthy
process, but it isn't difficult to master. The sweet, sticky
bananas coupled with a generous glug of rum,
complements the flaky chocolate pastry perfectly.

125 g/1 cup plain/all-
    purpose flour
35 g/¼ cup cocoa powder
a pinch of salt
2 teaspoons freshly
    squeezed lemon juice
50–75 ml/¼–⅓ cup cold
    water
125 g/1 stick cold butter
vanilla ice cream, to serve

**Banana caramel
topping**

100 g/½ cup caster/
    granulated sugar
2 tablespoons dark rum
60 g/5 tablespoons butter,
    cut into cubes
3 firm bananas, peeled and
    sliced

*a heavy-bottomed ovenproof
    frying pan/skillet about
    21 cm/8 in. in diameter*

Serves 8

To make the pastry, sift the flour and cocoa together in a large bowl and stir in
the salt. Make a well in the middle. Stir the lemon juice into the cold water and
add two-thirds of the mixture to the dry ingredients. Mix and knead until you
have a firm dough, adding more water if needed. This is called the *détrempe*.
Flatten it, wrap in clingfilm/plastic wrap and chill for at least an hour.

Put the butter in between 2 sheets of baking parchment and bash it with a
rolling pin until you have a flat rectangle of butter about 2-cm/¾-in. thick.

On a lightly floured surface, roll the *détrempe* into a rectangle, about 1.25-cm/
½-in. thick and place the butter in the centre. Fold the edges of the dough over
the butter to create a neat parcel. Turn the dough over, so the seams are
underneath, and roll into a neat rectangle of about 38 x 20 cm/16 x 8 in. With
a short edge facing you, brush off any excess flour and fold over the furthest
edge towards you and then the edge nearest you over the top. Seal the edges
together with your fingers. Dust the surface with more flour and turn the dough
90 degrees. Roll into a rectangle, brush off any excess flour and fold as before.
Seal the edges with your fingers, wrap the dough in clingfilm/plastic wrap and
rest in the fridge for an hour. Repeat the rolling, folding and resting twice more,
so in the end the dough will have been rolled and folded six times and rested in
the fridge three times. Chill in the fridge for at least 2 hours, the last time.

Preheat the oven to 200°C (400°F) Gas 6.

Put the sugar in an even layer in the frying pan/skillet. Add the rum and set over
a gentle heat until you have a rich golden caramel. You can swirl the pan
gently, but do not stir. You don't want it to be too dark at this stage, as it will be
cooked again in the oven. Remove from the heat and gently stir in the butter.

Roll the pastry out on a lightly floured surface to about the 3-mm/⅛-in. thick.
Cut out a circle slightly larger than the frying pan/skillet and set aside.

Arrange the bananas in concentric circles on top of the cooled caramel. Drape
the pastry over the top and tuck it in around the edges. Prick the pastry several
times with a fork and bake in the preheated oven for 30 minutes, or until the
pastry has puffed up. Cool the tarte in its pan for 5 minutes before inverting
onto a serving dish. Serve hot with vanilla ice cream.

chocolate and cinnamon buns

◆———————◆———————◆

These sticky spiced buns make the perfect afternoon treat. Soft, buttery and with a warming hit of spice, stopping at one requires a will of iron.

200 ml/³/₄ cup milk

1 vanilla pod/bean, seeds scraped out

550 g/4¹/₃ cups strong white bread flour

60 g/4 tablespoons butter

60 g/¹/₄ cup plus 1 tablespoon caster/granulated sugar

1 teaspoon salt

7 g/2¹/₄ teaspoons fast-acting yeast

1 whole egg plus 4 egg yolks

Cinnamon sugar filling

100 g/6¹/₂ tablespoons butter, melted

175 g/³/₄ cup plus 2 tablespoons light muscovado/brown sugar

1 tablespoon ground cinnamon

a pinch of salt

150 g/5 oz. dark/bittersweet chocolate (60–70% cocoa solids), finely chopped

Orange and ginger bun variation

1 tablespoon ground ginger

finely grated zest of 1 large orange

2 balls of stem ginger, finely chopped

an ovenproof baking dish, greased

Makes 12

Put the milk and vanilla in a saucepan set over a gentle heat to warm slightly. Sift the flour into a large bowl and rub in the butter with your fingertips. Stir in the sugar, salt and yeast. Make a well in the middle and pour in the warm milk, egg and egg yolks. Use a fork to beat the milk and eggs together and start bringing the dry ingredients into the wet until combined. It may take a little time for the flour to absorb all of the moisture, but keep mixing and it will happen. Once the mixture is fully combined, tip it onto an oiled work surface and knead for about 10 minutes, or until the dough is smooth, soft and springy. The dough should be moist but not sticky. Add a little more flour if the dough is too wet or a little water if too dry. Oil a large bowl and put the dough into it. Cover the top with clingfilm/plastic wrap and leave it to rise somewhere warm for about an hour, or until the dough has doubled in size.

Knock back the dough and turn it out onto a work surface to knead for another minute or so. Roll the dough into a large rectangle, about 5-mm/¹/₄-in. thick. Liberally paint the rectangle with melted butter, leaving a 2.5-cm/1-in. gap around the edges. Stir together the sugar, cinnamon and salt and sprinkle it evenly over the dough. Scatter the chopped chocolate over the cinnamon sugar in an even layer and gently press the filling into the dough.

Beginning with the longest edge, tightly roll the dough into a sausage. Pinch together the seam and roll the sausage over, seam side down. Cut the dough into 12 equal pieces. Arrange the rolls, next to each other, with a little gap between each one, cut-side down, in the prepared baking dish. Cover with a clean kitchen cloth and leave somewhere warm to rise again for about an hour, or until almost double in size.

Preheat the oven to 190°C (375°F) Gas 5.

Bake the buns for 20–25 minutes, or until golden brown and well risen – they are delicious served warm or cold.

Orange and ginger buns

Replace the ground cinnamon with a mixture of ground ginger, orange zest and stem ginger and follow the instructions as above for a fruity, chocolate orange take on these tasty buns.

Starter

½ teaspoon caster/
  granulated sugar
½ teaspoon plain/
  all-purpose flour
7 g/2¼ teaspoons fast-
  acting yeast
2 tablespoons warm water

Dough

125 ml/½ cup milk
25 g/2 tablespoons butter
50 g/¼ cup caster/
  granulated sugar
1 teaspoon salt
1 large egg
300 g/2⅓ cups strong white
  bread flour

Filling

200 g/6½ oz. unsweetened
  pistachio paste
150 g/¾ cup caster/
  granulated sugar
1 heaped tablespoon cocoa
  powder, sifted
60 ml/¼ cup milk
60 g/4 tablespoons butter
1 large egg yolk
1 teaspoon vanilla paste

Glaze

25 g/2 tablespoons butter,
  melted
1 teaspoon instant espresso
  dissolved in 1 tablespoon
  boiling water
1 tablespoon caster/
  granulated sugar

a 900-g/2-lb. loaf pan,
  greased

Serves 8–10

pistachio and chocolate povitica

Traditionally, this Eastern European bread is filled with
walnuts and spice. I have swapped the walnuts for
pistachios and spurned the spice in favour of chocolate.

Stir the starter ingredients together in a small bowl and cover the top with
clingfilm/plastic wrap. Leave for 5 minutes, or until the mixture is frothy and has
more than doubled in size.

In the meantime, put the milk in a saucepan set over a medium heat and stir until
the milk scalds. Pour the milk into a large bowl and stir in the butter until it has
melted. Leave to cool slightly. Whisk the sugar, salt and egg yolk into the milk
before stirring in the starter and sifting over half of the flour. Roughly combine
the ingredients with a fork, before sifting over half of the remaining flour. Turn
the dough out onto a lightly floured surface and knead until elastic and no
longer sticky. You may need to add the remaining flour, but you may not, it will
depend on the absorbency of the flour. The kneading takes time, so be patient.

Oil a large bowl and put the dough into it. Cover the top with clingfilm/plastic
wrap and leave it to rise somewhere warm for about an hour, or until the dough
has doubled in size. When ready, knock back the dough and turn it out onto a
work surface to knead for another minute or so. Roll the dough into a large
rectangle of about 50 x 30 cm/20 x 12 in.

To make the filling, simply mix together all of the ingredients into a thick paste.
Spread it evenly over the dough and carefully roll it up (like you would a swiss
roll/jellyroll) until you have one long sausage. Lift it carefully and let the weight
of either end stretch it a little longer.

Arrange the dough (with the join underneath), in a 'U' shape in the prepared
loaf pan, with a tail of dough hanging out of the pan on either side. Coil the
tails of dough in on themselves, tucking the ends in.

Make the glaze by mixing the melted butter and coffee together, and paint the
top of the loaf with the mixture. Sprinkle over the sugar, cover with a clean
kitchen cloth and leave to rise for another hour.

Preheat the oven to 180°C (350°F) Gas 4.

Bake for 15 minutes, then reduce the oven temperature to 150°C (300°F) Gas 2
and continue to bake for 30–45 minutes, or until done. Leave the povitica to
cool in its pan on top of a wire rack for 30 minutes before turning out.

choc chip brioche

250 g/2 cups white bread flour

60 g/¼ cup plus 1 tablespoon caster/granulated sugar

7 g/2¼ teaspoons fast-acting yeast

½ teaspoon salt

3 eggs

2 teaspoons vanilla paste

125 g/1 stick butter, at room temperature, cut into cubes

150 g/¾ cup dark/bittersweet chocolate chips (60–70% cocoa solids)

1 small beaten egg, for glazing

1 tablespoon pearl sugar (optional)

Brioche bread and butter pudding variation

75 g/5 tablespoons soft butter

300 g/10 oz. stale brioche, sliced and buttered

50 g/1½ oz. dark/bittersweet chocolate, roughly chopped

3 eggs

75 g/⅓ cup caster/granulated sugar

200 ml/¾ cup double/heavy cream

200 ml/¾ cup milk

1 teaspoon vanilla paste

60 ml/¼ cup dark rum

a 22-cm/9-in. fluted brioche pan, greased

Serves 6–8

Rich, buttery and with a tender crumb, this enriched French dough is slow to prove, but the results are definitely worth the wait – pudding heaven!

Put the flour, sugar, yeast and salt in a freestanding mixer fitted with a dough hook. Mix on a low speed to combine, before adding the eggs, one at a time. You may need to scrape round the bowl to ensure all the flour mixes properly with the eggs. Increase the speed to medium and add the vanilla. Add the butter, a little at a time. Once you have added all the butter, increase the speed to high and leave to mix for 7–8 minutes, or until the dough is glossy and elastic and starts to pull away from the edge of the bowl. This enriched dough is very sticky, so don't expect it to look like your average bread dough. Reduce the speed of the mixer to low again and add the chocolate chips.

Oil a large bowl and put the dough into it. Cover the top with clingfilm/plastic wrap and set in the fridge to rise for 7–14 hours, or overnight. When ready, knock back the dough and turn it out onto a floured surface to knead for another minute or so. Use a dough scraper to cut one-third of the dough off. With lightly floured hands, roll the two-thirds piece of dough into a ball and place it (working side down) in the prepared pan. Poke a hole the middle of the dough. Roll the smaller piece of dough into a second ball and pinch the base. Insert the pinched end into the hole in the larger ball of dough for the classic *Brioches Parisiennes* shape. Cover with a clean kitchen cloth and leave to rise at room temperature for 2–3 hours, or until the brioche has risen to just above the pan.

Preheat the oven to 180°C (350°F) Gas 4.

Glaze the top of the dough with the egg yolk and sprinkle with pearl sugar. Bake in the preheated oven for 20 minutes, then reduce the oven temperature to 160°C (325°F) Gas 3 and bake for a further 35–40 minutes, or until the brioche is deep golden and an inserted skewer comes out clean. Cool the brioche in its pan on top of a wire rack before turning out.

Brioche bread and butter pudding

Leftover brioche makes for a sensational bread and butter pudding. Preheat the oven to 160°C (325°F) Gas 3. Butter a baking dish and arrange the buttered brioche in it, butter side up. Scatter over the chopped chocolate. Whisk together the remaining ingredients and pour over the brioche. Place the dish inside a larger roasting pan and pour enough hot water to fill 2.5 cm/1 in. deep. Bake in the preheated oven for 30–40 minutes, or until just set and golden on top.

desserts

Indulgent and impressive, these
desserts ooze with both
chocolate and style

chocolate fondants

A fondant is definitely a contender for the perfect chocolate dessert. Add salted caramel and whomever you bake this for will be putty in your hands.

180 g/6 oz. dark/ bittersweet chocolate, (60–70% cocoa solids) broken into pieces

180 g/1½ sticks butter, cut into cubes

4 large eggs

150 g/¾ cup caster/ granulated sugar

90 g/¾ cup plain/ all-purpose flour

Salted caramel fondant variation

50 g/¼ cup light muscovado/brown sugar

100 ml/scant ½ cup double/heavy cream

1 teaspoon vanilla extract

¼ teaspoon salt

150 g/5 oz. dark/ bittersweet chocolate (60–70% cocoa solids), broken into pieces

150 g/10 tablespoons butter, cut into cubes

3 large eggs

125 g/⅔ cup caster/ granulated sugar

75 g/½ cup plus 1 tablespoon plain/ all-purpose flour

6 x 200-ml/6½-oz. ramekins, greased and dusted with cocoa powder then chilled

Makes 6

Put the chocolate and butter in a heatproof bowl suspended over a pan of barely simmering water and leave to melt, stirring every now and then. Leave the chocolate and butter to cool slightly.

In the meantime, whisk the eggs and sugar together until it reaches the ribbon stage – the mixture is pale yellow, thick and forms a ribbon when the whisk is lifted. Sift in half of the flour and fold in with a large metal spoon. Add half of the melted chocolate mixture and fold in. Repeat with the remaining flour, followed by the chocolate and fold until streak-free.

Arrange the prepared ramekins on a baking sheet. Divide the cake batter between the ramekins and chill in the fridge for 2 hours.

Preheat the oven to 200°C (400°F) Gas 6.

Bake the chilled fondants in the preheated oven for 11–13 minutes, or until a crust has formed on the tops and the sides are just starting to come away from the ramekins. Leave to stand for 1 minute before turning out.

Top tip
Once you have divided the mixture between the ramekins, the fondants can be frozen for up to 1 month and cooked from frozen, by simply adding an extra 5 minutes to the cooking time.

Salted caramel fondants
Add salted caramel to the fondant for added indulgence. To make the salted caramel. Simply put the light muscovado/brown sugar, cream, vanilla and salt in a saucepan set over a gentle heat and stir until the sugar has melted. Bring to the boil and continue to boil until the mixture has slightly thickened. Remove from the heat and leave to cool completely. Divide the caramel between six holes in an ice cube tray and freeze for 1–2 hours, or until completely set.

Make the fondant batter following the instructions above but reducing the quantities according to the salted caramel fondants ingredients.

Divide half of the cake batter between the prepared ramekins. Pop out the frozen cubes of caramel and place one in each ramekin. Top up with the remaining batter – they should only be three-quarters full. Chill, bake and turn out as above.

50 g/3 tablespoons butter

300 ml/1¼ cups milk

500 g/4 cups plain/all-purpose flour

1 teaspoon salt

75 g/scant ⅓ cup caster/granulated sugar

14 g/4½ teaspoons fast-acting yeast

2 egg yolks

1 teaspoon vanilla paste

sunflower oil, for frying

Chocolate glaze

100 g/3½ oz. dark/bittersweet chocolate, chopped

75 g/5 tablespoons butter

100 ml/scant ½ cup double/heavy cream

3 tablespoons golden/light corn syrup

Chocolate filled doughnut variation

400 ml/1⅔ cups milk

1 vanilla pod/bean, seeds scraped out

5 egg yolks

100 g/½ cup caster/granulated sugar

25 g/3 tablespoons cocoa powder, sifted

50 g/1½ oz. dark/bittersweet chocolate, melted

150 ml/⅔ cup double/heavy cream

a 7.5-cm/3-in. round cookie cutter

a baking sheet lined with baking parchment

a disposable piping/pastry bag (optional)

Makes about 16

chocolate glazed doughnuts

———◦———

Who can resist the allure of a freshly made doughnut? Deep-fried dough, dredged in sugar and filled with silky smooth chocolate crème pâtissière or formed into rings and coated in a dark and sticky chocolate glaze.

Put the butter and milk in a saucepan set over a gentle heat and stir until melted. Leave to cool until lukewarm. In the meantime, sift the flour into a large bowl and make a well in the middle. Add the salt to one side of the bowl and the sugar and yeast to the other. Pour two-thirds of the warm milk into the well, along with the egg yolks. Fork together the ingredients before turning the dough out onto a lightly floured surface. Knead for about 10 minutes (adding more of the milk if needed), or until the dough is soft and elastic. Oil a large bowl and put the dough into it. Cover the top with clingfilm/plastic wrap and leave it to rise somewhere warm for about an hour, or until the dough has doubled in size.

Once the dough has risen, knock it back and knead again a few times, before rolling it out on a lightly floured surface until about 1.25-cm/½-in. thick. Use the cookie cutter to cut out rounds. Insert your finger into the centre of each round and spin them to make a wide hole in the centre of each doughnut. Arrange the doughnuts on the prepared baking sheet, well spaced apart and cover with a clean kitchen cloth. Set in a warm place for about 30–45 minutes, or until the doughnuts have nearly doubled in size.

Meanwhile pour enough sunflower oil into a wide, heavy-bottomed saucepan so it is about 6-cm/2¼-in. deep. Heat the oil until it reaches 180°C (350°F), or until a breadcrumb dropped in the oil sizzles. Carefully place the doughnuts in the oil using a slotted spoon and cook for a few minutes on each side until golden brown. Cook the doughnuts in batches so as not to overcrowd the pan. Remove from the oil and drain on paper towels. Make the glaze by melting the ingredients together in a saucepan until smooth and glossy. Dunk the doughnuts in the glaze and set before eating. The doughnuts are best eaten on the day.

Chocolate filled doughnuts

If you prefer a filled doughnut to a glazed doughnut, skip the process for making holes in the centre and fry the doughnuts whole. Make the chocolate crème pâtissière following the instructions on page 91, but swap the cornflour for cocoa and leave out the butter. Whip the cream until stiff, but not dry and fold it into the chocolate crème pâtissière. Spoon the mixture in the piping/pastry bag and snip off the end. Pierce a hole in the side of each doughnut with a knife, push the tip of the piping/pastry bag into each doughnut and fill generously. Eat straight away.

white chocolate crème brûlée

Thick custard with a crunchy sugar topping, a crème brûlée is pure indulgence. I've given this classic a makeover with the addition of silky white chocolate.

1 vanilla pod/bean, seeds scraped out
600 ml/2½ cups double/heavy cream
8 egg yolks
50 g/¼ cup caster/granulated sugar, plus extra for sprinkling
100 g/3½ oz. white chocolate, melted

8 x 200-ml/6½-oz. ramekins set inside a roasting pan
a cook's blowtorch

Makes 8

Preheat the oven to 150°C (300°F) Gas 2.

Put the vanilla seeds and pod/bean in a saucepan with the cream set over a gentle heat and warm until it just comes to the boil. In the meantime, whisk the egg yolks and sugar together until pale and set a fine mesh sieve/strainer over the bowl. Pour the hot cream through the sieve into the egg mixture and whisk together. Discard the vanilla pod/bean. Whisk the melted white chocolate into the custard and divide the mixture between the ramekins.

Pour boiling water into the roasting pan until it reaches halfway up the ramekins and carefully put in the preheated oven. Bake for 35–40 minutes, or until the custards are just set, with a slight wobble in the middle.

Transfer the ramekins onto a wire rack and leave to cool. Once cold, pop the custards in the fridge for at least 4 hours, or overnight.

Sprinkle a fine layer of caster/granulated sugar over the top of each crème brûlée (about 1 teaspoon per custard). Caramelize the sugar using a cook's blowtorch or under a hot grill/broiler. Leave the caramel to harden and serve.

hot chocolate soufflé

Soufflés are always impressive, but are simpler to achieve than many people think. Make sure you preheat your oven and run your thumb around the inner rim of the ramekin before baking and your soufflés can't fail to rise.

500 ml/2 cups milk

1 vanilla pod/bean, seeds scraped out

6 eggs, separated

200 g/1 cup caster/granulated sugar

60 g/½ cup cornflour/cornstarch, sifted

65 g/½ cup cocoa powder, sifted

a pinch of salt

icing/confectioners' sugar, to dust (optional)

pouring cream or vanilla ice cream, to serve (optional)

6 x 200-ml/6½-oz. ramekins, greased and dusted with cocoa powder then chilled

Makes 6

Put the milk and vanilla pod/bean and seeds in a saucepan set over a gentle heat and slowly bring to the boil. In the meantime, whisk the egg yolks, 100 g/½ cup of the sugar, the cornflour/cornstarch and cocoa in a heatproof bowl to form a paste and set a fine mesh sieve/strainer over the top. Once the milk just comes to the boil, pour it over the egg mixture through the sieve/strainer. Discard the vanilla pod/bean and whisk the hot milk into the paste to make a custard, then return it to the saucepan and stir continuously until thickened slightly. Leave to cool.

Preheat the oven to 200°C (400°F) Gas 6.

Whisk the egg whites with a pinch of salt and gradually add the remaining sugar, a little at a time, to make a stiff and glossy meringue. Whisk the custard mixture until smooth and fold in the meringue, until streak-free, being careful not to knock the air out of the mixture.

Fill the ramekins to the top, level the surface with a palette knife and run your thumb around the rim of each ramekin. Place the ramekins on a baking sheet and bake in the preheated oven for 11–13 minutes, or until they are well risen. Do not open the oven door during baking or the soufflés may sink.

Dust with icing/confectioners' sugar if you wish and serve immediately with pouring cream or vanilla ice cream.

gâteau au marathon

·········•··•◦•··•·········

This layered gâteau is impossible to resist and is based on one of my favourite confections: the Snickers® bar or, as it was named in Britain during my youth, Marathon.

6 large eggs, separated
a pinch of salt
200 g/1 cup
    caster/granulated sugar
200 g/6½ oz. dark/
    bittersweet chocolate,
    melted and cooled
100 g/⅔ cup peanuts,
    blitzed in a food processor
3 tablespoons peanut oil

Peanut mousse

200 g/6½ oz. white
    chocolate, chopped
3 large eggs, separated
a pinch of salt
300 ml/1¼ cups double/
    heavy cream
5 heaped tablespoons
    smooth peanut butter
3 tablespoons caster/
    granulated sugar
3 gelatine leaves, soaked in
    cold water for 10 minutes
    (or 1½ teaspoons gelatine
    powder)
3 Snickers® bars, chopped
    into small pieces

Peanut caramel

250 g/8 oz. caramel sauce
25 g/2 tablespoons butter
a pinch of salt
100 g/⅔ cup salted peanuts

Ganache

100 g/3½ oz. dark/
    bittersweet chocolate,
    chopped
100 ml/scant ½ cup
    double/heavy cream

3 x 23-cm/9-in. shallow,
    loose-bottomed cake pans,
    greased
a 23-cm/9-in. deep cake
    pan, lined with food-safe
    acetate

Serves 10–12

Preheat the oven to 180°C (350°F) Gas 4.

To make the cake, put the egg whites and salt in a large bowl, whisk to stiff peaks and set aside. In a separate bowl, whisk the egg yolks and sugar together until the mixture is pale, mousse-like and leaves a ribbon trail when you lift the whisk. Fold in the cooled melted chocolate and the ground peanuts, then the oil. Beat in one-third of the stiff egg white. Fold the remaining egg whites into the chocolate mixture with a large metal spoon, until fully combined.

Divide the mixture between the shallow pans and bake in the preheated oven for 15–20 minutes, or until an inserted skewer comes out clean. Cool the cakes in their pans for 10 minutes before turning out to cool completely on wire racks.

To make the peanut mousse, melt the chocolate in a heatproof bowl set over a pan of barely simmering water. In the meantime, whisk the egg whites with the salt until stiff, but not dry. In a separate bowl, lightly whip the cream. Leave the chocolate to cool slightly, before whisking in the egg yolks, peanut butter and sugar. Scrape the peanut butter mixture into the whipped cream and whisk to combine. Squeeze the excess water from the gelatine and dissolve in 2 tablespoons of hot water. Add this to the peanut cream and whisk again. Fold the egg whites into the mixture with a large metal spoon. Be careful not to knock the air out of the mousse. Finally fold in the chopped Snickers® bars.

Push one of the cakes into the base of the deep cake ring. Pour over half of the mousse, level with a palette knife and gently press a second layer of cake on top. Pour over the rest of the mousse and top with the final layer of cake. Press down firmly and pop it in the fridge for a few hours to set.

To make the peanut caramel, put the caramel sauce, butter and salt into a pan and stir over a gentle heat until the butter has melted and the salt has dissolved. Bring to the boil, still stirring every now and then, until the mixture has thickened. Take the pan off the heat, stir in the peanuts and leave to cool, but not set. Pour over the top of the cake, level with a palette knife and return to the fridge.

Finally, make the ganache following the instructions on page 65, but using the quantities here. Leave to cool until thick enough to pour without running before spreading it evenly over the peanut caramel. Return to the fridge until set. Carefully slide off the cake ring and peel off the acetate and serve.

white chocolate and raspberry cheesecake

Few things are more pleasurable than a creamy baked cheesecake. Caramelizing white chocolate gives a sophisticated toffee depth, while the addition of fresh raspberries cuts through its sweetness beautifully.

150 g/5 oz. digestive biscuits/graham crackers

75 g/5 tablespoons butter, melted, plus extra for greasing

Filling

300 g/1 pint fresh raspberries

725 g/24 oz. full-fat cream cheese (such as Kraft Philadelphia)

300 g/1½ cup caster/ granulated sugar

a pinch of salt

25 g/3½ tablespoons cornflour/cornstarch

seeds of 2 vanilla pods/ beans (or 2 teaspoons vanilla paste)

250 g/8 oz. white chocolate, melted and cooled

3 eggs, plus 1 egg yolk

160 ml/⅔ cup sour cream

1 tablespoon freshly squeezed lemon juice

a 23-cm/9-in. deep loose-bottomed springform cake pan

Serves 8–10

For best results, make sure all of the filling ingredients are at room temperature before you begin.

Preheat the oven to 180°C (350°F) Gas 4.

Blitz the digestives/graham crackers in a food processor and add the melted butter and blitz again. Press the biscuit rubble firmly into the bottom of the prepared pan and bake in the preheated oven for 10 minutes. Leave to cool on a wire rack. Once cool, paint the inside of the pan liberally with melted butter and set on a baking sheet. Increase the oven to 220°C (425°F) Gas 7.

Put half of the raspberries on the cold biscuit base. Beat the cream cheese until creamy, before gradually adding 200 g/1 cup of the sugar, the cornflour/cornstarch and salt. Add the vanilla and chocolate, before whisking in the eggs and yolk, one at a time. Whisk in the sour cream and pour the mixture over the biscuit base. Bake in the preheated oven for 10 minutes. Reduce the oven to 110°C (225°F) Gas ¼.

Bake for a further 30–35 minutes. If you gently shake the pan, there should be a slight wobble in the middle. Turn off the oven and leave the cheesecake to cool in the oven for 2 hours with the oven door slightly ajar. Cover loosely with foil (without touching the top) and set in the fridge until ready to serve.

Put the remaining raspberries in a small pan with the lemon juice and remaining 100 g/½ cup of sugar and set over a gentle heat. Stir until the berries break down, then bring to the boil. Pass the mixture through a fine mesh sieve/strainer to remove the seeds and leave to cool.

Carefully remove the cheesecake from the pan and slide it onto a serving plate. Swirl the raspberry coulis over the top of the cheesecake.

Caramelized white chocolate cheesecake

Leave out the raspberries and caramelize the white chocolate for a simpler version of this cheesecake. Preheat the oven to 120°C (250°F) Gas ½. Put the chocolate on a baking sheet and bake for 45 minutes–1 hour, stirring every 10 minutes, until pale golden brown. If the chocolate looks chalky or seized, simply continue to stir until it is smooth again. Cover and set aside until needed.

chocolate and berry crumble

A failsafe British pudding with the glamorous addition of cocoa, this crumble is simple to knock up and especially delicious doused in hot vanilla custard.

500 g/1 lb. mixed berries (raspberries, blackberries, blueberries, etc.)
1 tablespoon caster/granulated sugar
seeds of 1 vanilla pod/bean
custard, to serve (optional)

Crumble
200 g/1¾ cups plain/all-purpose flour
25 g/3½ tablespoons cocoa powder
a pinch of salt
100 g/6½ tablespoons cold butter, cut into cubes
100 g/½ cup caster/granulated sugar

a 25-cm/10-in. square baking dish

Serves 8–10

Put the berries in the baking dish. Sprinkle over the sugar, add the vanilla and toss everything together until the fruit is evenly coated.

For the crumble, sift the flour, cocoa and salt together in a large bowl and mix together until well combined. Add the butter and rub the mixture lightly between your fingers and thumbs until it resembles coarse breadcrumbs. Stir through the sugar and tip the crumble over the fruit, but do not press it down.

Bake in the preheated oven for 35–40 minutes, or until the top is golden and the fruit is soft and bubbling. Leave the crumble to cool for 15–20 minutes before serving with lashings of custard.

chocolate marquise

This impressive and simple make-ahead dessert is a sure-fire winner. I like to serve mine in thick slices with a generous scattering of seasonal fruit.

300 g/10 oz. dark/ bittersweet chocolate (60–70% cocoa solids), broken into pieces
150 g/10 oz. butter, cut into cubes
a generous pinch of salt
5 large egg yolks
150 g/^{3}/4 cup caster/ granulated sugar
1 teaspoon vanilla paste
500 ml/2 cups double/ heavy cream
seasonal fruit, to serve

a 1-litre/-quart terrine, oiled and lined with clingfilm/plastic wrap

Serves 8

Put the chocolate, butter and salt in a heatproof bowl suspended over a pan of barely simmering water and leave to melt, stirring every now and then with a rubber spatula.

In the meantime, put the egg yolks, sugar and vanilla in a large heatproof bowl and, using a handheld electric whisk, whisk until pale, thick and mousse-like. This can take some time, so be patient. Transfer the bowl to a pan of barely simmering water and continue to whisk until the mixture is hot, taking care not to curdle the eggs. Remove the bowl from the heat, pour the melted chocolate and butter down the side and whisk together. Leave to cool.

Whisk the cream until stiff, but not dry and carefully fold it into the chocolate mixture with a large metal spoon until streak-free. Pour the mixture into the prepared terrine and cover with clingfilm/plastic wrap. Transfer to the fridge to set overnight. You can make this up to three days before you want to serve it.

Once set, unwrap the terrine and upturn it onto a serving plate. Dip a palette knife in boiling water and wipe dry before running it over the top and sides of the marquise to give it a smooth, glossy surface. Use a hot knife to cut generous slices and serve with seasonal fruit.

150 g/5 oz. digestive biscuits/graham crackers

2 tablespoons cocoa powder

1 teaspoon ground cinnamon

75 g/5 tablespoons butter, melted, plus extra for greasing

Filling

725 g/24 oz. full-fat cream cheese (such as Kraft Philadelphia)

200 g/1 cup caster/granulated sugar

25 g/3½ tablespoons cornflour/cornstarch

1 teaspoon ground cinnamon

a pinch of salt

seeds of 2 vanilla pods/beans

3 whole eggs, plus 1 yolk

160 ml/⅔ cup sour cream

200 g/6½ oz. dark/bittersweet chocolate, melted and cooled

Chocolate and chilli/chile variation

200 g/6½ oz. chilli/chile-flavoured dark/bittersweet chocolate, melted and cooled

½ teaspoon chilli/hot red pepper powder

candied chillies/chiles (see page 145)

a 23-cm/9-in. deep loose-bottomed springform cake pan

Serves 8–10

dark chocolate and cinnamon cheesecake

This baked cheesecake has the added sophistication of a generous helping of dark/bittersweet chocolate. Either spiced with cinnamon or with an added kiss of chilli/chile heat, this cheesecake will have you fighting over the final slice.

For best results, make sure all of the filling ingredients are at room temperature before you begin.

Preheat the oven to 180°C (350°F) Gas 4.

First, blitz the digestives/graham crackers, cocoa and cinnamon in a food processor, add the melted butter and blitz again. Press the biscuit rubble firmly into the bottom of the pan and bake for 10 minutes. Leave to cool on a wire rack. Once cool, paint the inside of the pan liberally with melted butter and set on a baking sheet. Increase the oven to 220°C (425°F) Gas 7.

Beat the cream cheese until creamy, before gradually adding the sugar, cornflour/cornstarch, cinnamon and salt. Add the vanilla, before whisking in the eggs and yolk, one at a time. Whisk in the sour cream and cooled melted chocolate and pour the mixture over the biscuit base. Bake for 10 minutes. Reduce the oven to 110°C (225°F) Gas ¼.

Bake for a further 25 minutes. If you gently shake the pan, there should be a slight wobble in the middle. Turn off the oven and leave the cheesecake to cool in the oven for 2 hours with the oven door slightly ajar.

Cover loosely with foil (without touching the top) and set in the fridge for 8 hours or overnight.

Dust the top with cinnamon and carefully remove the cheesecake from the pan and slide it onto a serving plate.

Chocolate and chilli/chile cheesecake

First, make the candied chillies/chiles following the instructions on page 145. Replace the cinnamon with chilli/hot red pepper powder, swap the chocolate with chilli/chile-flavoured dark chocolate and prepare as above. Sprinkle with candied chilli/chile and serve.

chocolate christmas pudding

100 g/½ cup light muscovado/brown sugar

100 g/6½ tablespoons butter, chopped

100 g/3½ oz. dark/bittersweet chocolate (60–70% cocoa solids), broken into pieces

120 g/1 scant cup dried sour cherries

40 g/¼ cup each of (dark) raisins and sultanas/golden raisins

75 g/½ cup Zante currants

25 g/2½ tablespoons dried cranberries

150 g/1 generous cup stoned/pitted prunes, chopped

2 balls of stem ginger, finely chopped

150 ml/⅔ cup brandy

100 ml/scant ½ cup port

50 ml/3 tablespoons Cointreau

grated zest and freshly squeezed juice of 2 oranges

1 vanilla pod/bean, seeds scraped out

1 large egg, beaten

50 g/⅓ cup blanched hazelnuts, roughly chopped

100 g/¾ cup plain/all-purpose flour

50 g/scant ½ cup cocoa powder

1 teaspoon each of mixed/apple pie spice, ground cinnamon and ginger

½ teaspoon freshly grated nutmeg

a pinch of salt

a 900-g/2-lb. pudding bowl, greased and base-lined with baking parchment

Serves 8

Christmas pudding is traditionally made on 'Stir-up Sunday' – the last Sunday before the beginning of Advent. Each family member takes a turn stirring the mixture and making a wish before the pudding is steamed, but you may find your wishes have already come true, with the addition of a hearty dose of chocolate into the mixture.

Put the sugar, butter, chocolate, dried fruits, stem ginger and alcohol in a saucepan and stir over a gentle heat until the chocolate and butter have melted. Bring to the boil and immediately turn off the heat. Stir in the orange zest and juice and vanilla, and leave to cool.

Once cool, mix in the beaten egg and hazelnuts before sifting in the flour, cocoa, spices and salt. Fold the dry ingredients into the wet until well mixed. Spoon the mixture into the prepared pudding bowl and smooth over the top.

Cut out a 33-cm/13-in. circle of baking parchment. Pleat the circle and place over the pudding. Cover with a lid made from a pleated circle of foil, then wrap string twice around the basin and tie to secure the paper and foil. Use more string to wrap over and under the bowl and tie a knot to make a handle.

Put the basin in the top of a steamer of simmering water for 3 hours. Top up with boiling water every hour, to prevent the pan from boiling dry. Alternatively, place the pudding on a trivet (or upturned, ovenproof dish) in a large saucepan. Add enough boiling water to come two-thirds up the side of the bowl. Cover with a well fitting lid and simmer for 2 hours, topping up the water every now and then to prevent the pan from boiling dry.

Once cool, unwrap the pudding and re-wrap. This way you can ensure that no water has got inside. Cover the cold pudding tightly with foil and store in a cool, dark place, preferably for at least a month, until ready to reheat.

At Christmas, steam the pudding over a pan of barely simmering water for 1½ hours to reheat, before turning the pudding out and pouring flaming brandy over the top. Serve with generous lashings of brandy butter.

Merry Christmas!

chocolate mince pies

Christmas feels incomplete without mince pies and chocolate, so in sybarite fashion, I have combined the two to create a satisfyingly luxurious take on a festive classic.

150 g/1 cup dried cranberries

100 g/²/₃ cup dried sour cherries

75 g/¹/₂ cup Zante currants

125 g/1 scant cup (dark) raisins

50 g/¹/₃ cup each of sultanas/golden raisins, finely chopped mixed citrus peel and dark/bittersweet chocolate

2 balls of stem ginger, finely chopped

1 small apple, peeled and finely chopped

85 g/6 tablespoons butter

30 g/¹/₄ cup blanched hazelnuts, chopped

150 g/³/₄ cup dark muscovado/brown sugar

grated zest and freshly squeezed juice of 2 oranges

50 ml/3 tablespoons port

1 teaspoon each of ground cinnamon, mixed/apple pie spice, ground ginger

seeds of 1 vanilla pod/bean

200 ml/1 scant cup brandy

1 beaten egg, for glazing

icing/confectioners' sugar, for dusting

Pastry

250 g/2 cups plain/all-purpose flour, sifted

a pinch of salt

100 g/6¹/₂ tablespoons cold butter, cut into cubes

100 g/¹/₂ cup caster/granulated sugar

1 egg, beaten

a 10-cm/4-in. round cookie cutter

a star-shaped cookie cutter

a 12-hole muffin pan

Makes 12

To make the mincemeat, place all of the ingredients, except for the brandy, in a large saucepan and place over a gentle heat. Stir until the sugar, chocolate and butter have melted. Leave to simmer for 10–15 minutes and then turn off the heat and leave to cool before stirring in the brandy. Use immediately or spoon into a large sterilized glass jar, topped with a disc of waxed paper. Store the mincemeat in a cool, dark place. The flavours will improve after a month or two, but the mincemeat will last up to one year. This makes far more than is needed for 12 mince pies, but it will be just enough to last the Christmas period. Once opened, store the mincemeat in the fridge.

To make the pastry, sift the flour into a large bowl and stir in the salt. Add the butter and rub the butter into the flour with your fingertips. Stir in the sugar and make a well in the middle of the bowl. Add the egg and use a fork to mix the dry ingredients into the wet. Tip the mixture out onto a lightly floured surface and lightly knead until it comes together into a dough. Wrap in clingfilm/plastic wrap and pop in the fridge to chill for 30 minutes.

Preheat the oven to 200°C (375°F) Gas 5.

Roll the pastry out on a lightly floured surface no thicker than 5 mm/¹/₄ in. Use the round cutter to stamp out 12 pastry discs. Line the muffin pan with the pastry discs and generously fill each one with mincemeat. Bring the rest of the pastry back together and re-roll. Use the star-shaped cutter to stamp out 12 stars and rest one on top of each pie to make an attractive lid.

Brush the top of each pie with a little beaten egg and bake in the preheated oven for 15–20 minutes, or until the pies are golden brown. Leave the pies to cool before taking them out of the pan. Lightly dust with icing/confectioners' sugar before serving.

matcha mousse cakes

Light and fluffy green tea sponge topped with chocolate
and ginger mousse; this is a showstopper of a dessert
to wow your lucky guests with.

2 balls of stem ginger, finely
sliced, plus extra to serve

Green tea cake

3 large eggs
90 g/scant ½ cup caster/
granulated sugar
20 g/4 teaspoons butter,
melted
2 teaspoons matcha
(green tea powder)
90 g/⅔ cup plain/
all-purpose flour

**Chocolate and
ginger mousse**

150 g/5 oz. dark/
bittersweet chocolate,
chopped
100 g/6½ tablespoons
butter
3 eggs, separated
6 tablespoons ginger syrup
(from a jar of stem ginger)
a pinch of salt
90 ml/⅓ cup plus
1 tablespoon double/
heavy cream

a 23 x 33-cm/9 x 13-in.
cake pan, lined with
baking parchment
8 x 4 x 6-cm/16⅝ x 2⅜-in.
ring moulds, greased with
a tasteless oil
a baking sheet lined with
baking parchment

Makes 8

Preheat the oven to 180°C (350°F) Gas 4.

To make the green tea cake, put the eggs and sugar in a large heatproof bowl
set over a pan of barely simmering water and whisk continuously until the
mixture is hot. Carefully remove the bowl from the heat and continue to whisk
vigorously until the mixture has doubled in volume and is at the ribbon stage
– pale, thick and mousse-like, leaving a slowly disappearing trail when you lift
the whisk. This can take 5 minutes with a handheld electric whisk, so be patient.

Pour the melted butter down the outer edge of the bowl and whisk in. Sift in the
matcha and flour and fold in using a large metal spoon, being careful not to
over mix and knock the air out of the batter. Pour the batter into the prepared
pan and gently level it with a palette knife. Bake in the preheated oven for
10–15 minutes, or until the cake is firm and springy to touch. Leave to cool
completely on a wire rack.

To make the chocolate and ginger mousse, melt the chocolate and butter
together in a heatproof bowl suspended over a pan of barely simmering water.
Once smooth, glossy and fully melted, leave to cool slightly before whisking
in the egg yolks and ginger syrup. In a separate bowl, whisk the egg whites
with the salt until stiff peaks form and fold into the chocolate mixture with a
large metal spoon. Be careful not to knock the air out of the mousse. In the
same bowl as you whisked the egg whites, whisk the cream to soft peaks
(there's no need to wash the beaters) and fold the cream into the mousse.
Decant into a jug/pitcher ready for assembling the mousse cakes.

To assemble, use the oiled rings to cut out a round of cake to fit the base of each
mould. Place the cake-filled ring moulds on the prepared baking sheet and
gently press the cake to ensure it is pushed fully down to the base. Top the cakes
with some fine slices of ginger before filling the rings with the mousse, right up
to their tops. Tap the baking sheet on the work surface gently to expel any air
bubbles. Put in the fridge to set for at least 6 hours, or overnight.

Before removing the ring moulds, artfully place a few matchsticks of ginger on
top. Place a mousse cake on an upturned egg cup before flashing round the
edge with a cook's blowtorch. You should be able to slide the ring mould down
off the cake. If you don't have a blowtorch, you can use a hairdryer or the heat
of your hands. Transfer to a plate using a palette knife and repeat.

petits fours

Bite-sized morsels of
chocolate deliciousness to
enjoy as after-dinner treats

chocolate and whisky truffles

◆———————◆———————◆

Making chocolate truffles is child's play, but all who you
serve them to will think you're a culinary alchemist.

150 g/5 oz. dark/
   bittersweet chocolate
   (60–70% cocoa solids),
   chopped
25 g/2 tablespoons butter,
   cut into small pieces
150 ml/²/₃ cup double/
   heavy cream
2 tablespoons light
   muscovado/brown sugar
1–2 tablespoons whisky
20 g/3 tablespoons cocoa
   powder

**Lime and chilli/chile
truffle variation**

finely grated zest of
   1½ limes
150 g/5 oz. chilli/chile-
   flavoured dark/bittersweet
   chocolate (60–70% cocoa
   solids), tempered (see page
   31)
finely grated zest of ½ lime

**Candied chillies/
chiles (optional)**

150 g/³/₄ cup
   caster/granulated sugar
2 fresh, long, red, hot
   chillies/chiles, deseeded
   and finely sliced

Each makes 25

Put the chopped chocolate and butter in a heatproof bowl and set aside. Put
the cream and sugar in a saucepan set over a gentle heat, stirring constantly
until the sugar has dissolved. Increase the heat and once it just comes to the
boil, turn off the heat and leave it to cool for 1 minute before pouring over the
chocolate. Mix with a rubber spatula until the chocolate melts and you are left
with a smooth, glossy ganache. Whisk in the whisky, a little at a time, tasting
between each addition. Leave the ganache to set at room temperature for
a few hours.

Sift the cocoa in a wide, shallow dish and set aside.

Once very firm, use a melon baller or teaspoon to scoop out even spoonfuls
of the ganache and roll between your palms to create balls. Roll the balls in the
cocoa, shake off the excess and arrange on a serving dish.

Lime and chilli/chile truffles

When you're used to making chocolate and whisky truffles, why not try
something a little more fiery? First, make the candied chilli/chile. Stir the sugar
and 150 ml/²/₃ cup of water in a saucepan set over a gentle heat until the
sugar has dissolved. Increase the heat and leave to boil for a minute or so.
Add the finely sliced chillies/chiles and reduce the heat, before leaving to
simmer very gently for 25 minutes. Turn off the heat and leave the chilli/chile
syrup to cool. Once cool, cover the top of the pan with clingfilm/plastic wrap
and leave to infuse and soak for at least 10 hours. You can make these up to
3 days before using.

For the truffles, follow the instructions above using chilli/chile-flavoured
chocolate, but omit the whisky and whisk lime zest into the ganache before
leaving to set. Once you've rolled the ganache into balls, arrange them on a
plate topped with baking parchment and chill in the fridge for 1 hour to firm up.

Dip the truffles in the tempered chocolate, until evenly coated, and place on a
piece of baking parchment. Decorate with a little candied chilli/chile and lime
zest and leave to set at room temperature for about 30 minutes before serving.

nougat

Sticky, chewy and dangerously moreish, these little squares of nougat are ideal to serve alongside an after dinner coffee or digestif.

300 g/1¹⁄₂ cups caster/ granulated sugar

50 g/3 tablespoons runny honey

50 g/3 tablespoons liquid glucose (or light corn syrup)

2 large egg whites

a pinch of salt

1 teaspoon vanilla paste

75 g/2¹⁄₂ oz. dark/ bittersweet chocolate (60–70% cocoa solids), roughly chopped

100 g/²⁄₃ cup dried cherries

100 g/²⁄₃ cup shelled unsalted pistachios

Chocolate, hazelnut and ginger nougat variation

100 g/²⁄₃ cup blanched hazelnuts

3 balls of stem ginger, finely chopped

Each makes about 25

Put the sugar, honey, liquid glucose and 100 ml/scant ¹⁄₂ cup of water in a saucepan set over a gentle heat. Do not stir and wait for the sugar to dissolve. You can use a pastry brush dipped in water to brush any sugar off the sides of the pan to prevent any crystallization. Once the sugar has completely dissolved, increase the heat slightly and simmer until the mixture reaches 160°C (320°F) – the hard crack stage (see page 73).

When the syrup starts to creep up to temperature, whisk the egg whites with the salt until stiff but not dry. Slowly pour in the syrup, whisking all the time. Once all the syrup has been incorporated, add the vanilla, increase the speed and continue whisking until the mixture is extremely thick and has cooled slightly. Fold in the chocolate, cherries and pistachios and spoon the mixture onto a sheet of baking parchment. Press a second sheet of baking parchment on top and use a rolling pin to press and roll it level to about 1-cm/³⁄₈-in. thick. Leave the nougat to set for a few hours until completely cold and firm.

Remove the top layer of baking parchment and turn the nougat over onto a chopping board. Peel off the base layer of baking parchment and use a sharp knife to cut the nougat into 5 x 2.5-cm/2 x 1-in. batons.

Chocolate, hazelnut and ginger nougat
Follow the instructions as above but replace the cherries and pistachios with hazelnuts and stem ginger.

150 g/³/₄ cup caster/
  granulated sugar
40 g/2½ tablespoons liquid
  glucose (or light corn
  syrup)
2 large egg whites
a pinch of salt
4 leaves of gelatine, soaked
  in cold water for
  10 minutes to soften
  (or 2 teaspoons
  gelatine powder)
50 g/1½ oz. dark/
  bittersweet chocolate
  (60–70% cocoa solids),
  melted and cooled, for
  drizzling
cocoa powder, to dust
1 tablespoon cocoa nibs
  (optional)

Chocolate-coated violet marshmallow variation

a few drops of violet extract
a little violet food colouring
  paste (I use Wilton's)
200 g/6½ oz. melted and
  cooled dark/bittersweet
  chocolate (60–70% cocoa
  solids), for dipping
10 g/2 tablespoons
  crystallized violet petal
  pieces (available online)

*a 18-cm/7-in. square cake
pan greased, lined with
oiled baking parchment
and liberally dusted with
icing/confectioners' sugar*

Each makes 20

chocolate marshmallows

Marshmallows are deceptively simple to make, but you'll gain the status of culinary wizard once you master these.

Put the sugar, liquid glucose and 100 ml/scant ½ cup of water in a small saucepan set over a gentle heat. Without stirring, leave the sugar to dissolve. You can use a pastry brush dipped in water to brush any sugar off the sides of the pan to prevent any crystallization. Once the sugar has completely dissolved, increase the heat slightly and simmer until the syrup reaches 125°C (250°F) – the 'hard-ball' stage.

Meanwhile, whisk the egg whites and salt together until stiff but not dry. Then, carefully, while continuing to whisk, pour the syrup into the bowl. Once all the syrup is incorporated, add the drained gelatine leaves, one at a time, whisking all the time. Continue to whisk the marshmallow mixture until it is completely cold. It is easiest to do this using a freestanding mixer, rather than a handheld electric whisk.

Once the mixture is cool enough so you can touch the bowl with your hand, whisk in 50 g/1½ oz. of the cool, melted chocolate until streak-free. Continue to whisk until the mixture is cold. Pour the mixture into the prepared cake pan and, using a palette knife dipped in boiling water, smooth over the surface. Dust the top with cocoa. Cover with clingfilm/plastic wrap (ensuring it does not touch the marshmallow mixture) and leave to set at room temperature for at least 3 hours, or overnight. Do not put the marshmallow in the fridge.

Once set, turn the marshmallow out onto a chopping board. Dust off any excess cocoa and drizzle with the remaining cooled melted chocolate before scattering over some cocoa nibs (if using). Leave to set before slicing into cubes.

Chocolate-coated violet marshmallows

For a dainty alternative to these chocolate marshmallows replace the 50 g/ 1½ oz. of the cool, melted chocolate and whisk in the violet extract and food colouring until streak-free. Before cutting, dunk each cube in the cool, melted chocolate, tap off the excess and place on a sheet of baking parchment. Sprinkle over the crystallized violet and leave to set at room temperature.

spiced chocolate fudge

Delicious, melt in the mouth chocolate fudge requires minimum effort and yields irresistible results.

½ teaspoon ground cinnamon

½ teaspoon ground ginger

¼ teaspoon freshly grated nutmeg

¼ teaspoon ground cardamom

a pinch of ground black pepper

850 ml/3½ cups double/ heavy cream

500 g/2½ cups caster/ granulated sugar

150 ml/⅔ cup liquid glucose (or light corn syrup)

100 g/6½ tablespoons butter

a pinch of salt

200 g/6½ oz. dark/ bittersweet chocolate (60–70% cocoa solids), melted and cooled

a 20-cm/8-in. square cake pan lined with baking parchment

Makes 64

Put everything except for the chocolate in a heavy-bottomed saucepan set over a gentle heat and stir until the sugar and butter have melted. Stop stirring and increase the heat slightly and leave to softly boil until the mixture reaches 120°C (250°F). Do not be tempted to crank the heat up to maximum to speed up the process, or you'll burn the fudge.

Remove the pan from the heat and leave to cool to 110°C (230°F), before stirring in the chocolate. Whisk gently until the mixture cools to 60°C (140°F), before pouring the chocolate fudge mixture into the prepared pan. Level the top with a palette knife and leave to set for a few hours before cutting into 2.5-cm/ 1-in. squares.

Chocolate fudge
If you'd rather make straightforward buttery fudge, you can simply omit the spices from the mixture and follow the instructions as above.

lamingtons

2 large eggs

65 g/⅓ cup caster/
granulated sugar

65 g/½ cup plain/
all-purpose flour

15 g/1 tablespoon melted
butter

finely grated zest of 1 lemon

Soaking syrup

freshly squeezed juice of 1
lemon

50 g/¼ cup caster/
granulated sugar

Coating

100 g/3½ oz. dark/
bittersweet chocolate
(60–70% cocoa solids),
chopped

100 ml/scant ½ cup
single/light cream

50 ml/3 tablespoons milk

150 g/1 generous cup
desiccated/shredded
coconut

**Sesame and white
chocolate lamington
variation**

20 ml/4 teaspoons toasted
sesame oil

200 g/7 oz. white chocolate,
chopped, to coat

65 ml/4 tablespoons single/
light cream, to coat

1 tablespoon toasted
sesame oil

150 g/1 cup toasted sesame
seeds

*a 13-cm/5-in. square cake
pan, greased and lined
with baking parchment*

Makes 16

Lamingtons are Australian cakes made from cubes of light fluffy sponge coated in chocolate and dunked in coconut. Add zesty lemon for extra zing or try my sesame and white chocolate lamingtons for a modern twist.

Preheat the oven to 190°C (375°F) Gas 5.

To make the cake batter, simply whisk the eggs and sugar together in a large heatproof bowl set over a pan of barely simmering water until the mixture is just warm. Take the bowl off the heat and continue to whisk until the eggs and sugar have at least doubled in volume and are pale and mousse-like. This can take some time, so be patient. Sift in the flour and fold in using a large metal spoon. Pour the melted butter down the side of the bowl and carefully fold it in followed by the lemon zest. Pour the batter into the prepared pan and level the top.

Bake in the preheated oven for 12–15 minutes, or until an inserted skewer comes out clean. While the cake is baking, stir together the lemon juice and sugar for the soaking syrup. Once the cake is hot out of the oven, stab the cake all over with a skewer and evenly pour all the syrup over the top.

Leave the cake to cool in its pan on top of a wire rack until completely cold before turning out.

To make the coating, simply place the chopped chocolate in a heatproof bowl and heat the cream and milk until it just reaches boiling point. Leave the cream to stand for 1 minute before pouring it over the chopped chocolate. Leave to stand for 30 seconds before gently stirring with a rubber spatula until all the chocolate has melted. Put the coconut in a wide, shallow dish and set aside.

Cut the cake into even squares. Spear each square with a fork and dunk it in the coating, tap off the excess and roll it in the desiccated/shredded coconut. Leave to set on a sheet of baking parchment for at least an hour.

Sesame and white chocolate lamingtons
Replace the butter with sesame oil in the cake batter. Add the sesame oil to the coating, replace the dark/bittersweet chocolate with white chocolate and swap the desiccated/shredded coconut with toasted sesame seeds

french fancies

...........•••••○●○•••••..........

Dainty squares of light sponge, topped with buttercream and enrobed in chocolate icing. These cute petits fours can't fail to tempt your guests.

60 g/½ stick soft butter

60 g/⅓ cup light muscovado/brown sugar

1 large egg, beaten

45 g/⅓ cup self-raising/ rising flour, sifted

15 g/2 tablespoons cocoa powder, sifted

½ teaspoon baking powder

a pinch of salt

a splash of milk, if needed

35 g/1 oz. white chocolate, melted and cooled, to decorate

16 chocolate coffee beans, to decorate (optional)

Soaking syrup

50 g/¼ cup caster/ granulated sugar

50 ml/3 tablespoons bourbon

Buttercream

20 g/1 tablespoon plus 1 teaspoon soft butter

40 g/⅓ cup icing/ confectioners' sugar, sifted

2 teaspoons bourbon

Chocolate icing

1 tablespoon bourbon

1 tablespoon golden syrup/ light corn syrup

365 g/3⅓ cups icing/ confectioners' sugar, sifted

40 g/1½ oz. dark/ bittersweet chocolate, finely chopped

1 teaspoon glycerine

a 12.5-cm/5-in. square cake pan, greased and base-lined with baking parchment

a disposable piping/pastry bag

Makes 16

Preheat the oven to 180°C (350°F) Gas 4.

To make the sponge, simply whisk the butter, light muscovado/brown sugar, egg, flour, cocoa, baking powder and salt together until light and fluffy. You can add milk to slightly slacken the mixture, if necessary. Spoon the mixture into the prepared cake pan and level the top with a palette knife. Bake in the preheated oven for 20 minutes, or until an inserted skewer comes out clean.

While the cake is baking, make the syrup. Simply put the sugar and bourbon into a small saucepan with 25 ml/1½ tablespoons of water and stir over a gentle heat until the sugar has dissolved. Once baked, stab the hot cake all over with a skewer and brush over the syrup. Leave the cake to cool completely, then transfer to the freezer for 30 minutes before cutting into 16 equal squares.

To make the buttercream, simply whisk the ingredients together until light and fluffy. Spoon into the piping/pastry bag and snip off the end. Squeeze a modest mound of buttercream in the centre on each square of cake. Pop the cakes back into the freezer to chill until the buttercream has hardened.

To make the chocolate icing, put the bourbon, golden/light corn syrup and 75 ml/⅓ cup of water in a saucepan set over a gentle heat and stir until melted. Continue to cook for 2–3 minutes before taking off the heat and stirring in the chocolate and glycerine until completely melted and glossy. Leave to cool until just warm – if the icing is too hot, the buttercream will melt.

Dunk each cake square, buttercream side down, into the chocolate icing, tap off the excess and place in petit four cases. Press the sides of the petit four cases into the unset icing and leave to set completely. Once set, drizzle some melted white chocolate over the top of each cake and set before serving.

Espresso French fancies

For an alcohol-free version of these chocolate French fancies, replace the bourbon in the soaking syrup with 2 teaspoons of instant espresso powder, the bourbon in the buttercream with 1 teaspoon of instant espresso powder dissolved in 2 teaspoons of boiling water and the dark/bittersweet chocolate in the chocolate icing with milk/semi-sweet chocolate. Drizzle with dark/bittersweet chocolate to contrast the white chocolate of the bourbon-flavoured fancies and decorate with chocolate coffee beans.

chocolate port shots

—◇—

Rich, indulgent and boozy, these chocolate and port
shots make the perfect after dinner treat.

100 g/3½ oz. dark/
  bittersweet chocolate
  (60–70% cocoa solids),
  chopped
100 ml/scant ½ cup
  double/heavy cream
1 tablespoon light
  muscovado/brown sugar
100 ml/scant ½ cup port
2 large egg yolks

Topping

75 ml/⅓ cup double/heavy
  cream
1 level tablespoon icing/
  confectioners' sugar, sifted
½ teaspoon vanilla paste
15 g/½ oz. dark/
  bittersweet chocolate
  (60–70% cocoa solids),
  shaved with a vegetable
  peeler, to decorate

*60-ml/2-oz. shot glasses
  or espresso cups*

Makes 6

To make the shots, put all of the ingredients except for the egg yolks in a small
saucepan set over a gentle heat and whisk until everything has melted.

Take the pan off the heat and leave to cool for a few minutes before whisking
in the egg yolks.

Divide the mixture between the shot glasses or espresso cups and leave them
to cool to room temperature before transferring them to the fridge for 4 hours,
or until completely set.

To make the topping, whisk the cream, icing/confectioners' sugar and vanilla
together until stiff but not dry and top each port shot with a dollop of it. Scatter
over a few chocolate shavings and return to the fridge until ready to eat.

Serve each shot with a small teaspoon.

Index

Acknowledgments

I am so very proud of this book, not least because pregnancy has made the process more challenging than I ever expected. Every recipe has been at least triple tested and I am so very grateful to the friends and family who helped along the way. A big hug of thanks must go to my marvellous mother, Lesley, for all her help and encouragement, especially when recipe deadlines were tight and morning sickness felt endless. Thanks too to the gorgeous love of my life, Richard, for never failing to make me laugh and for being my rock. Huge and heartfelt thanks to my little army of test bakers who gave such excellent feedback: Lauren Barnett, Georgina Cannon, Jane Carnall, Lisa Flanagan, Barbara Gebala, Deborah Glass, Rosie Ifould, Georgina Panton, Milli Taylor, Alys Torrance, Susan Wilk and Rebecca Woods.

Thanks must go to my wonderful agent, Olivia Guest, for all her support and to the amazing team at Ryland Peters & Small for helping to create such a beautiful book. Huge thanks to Mitzie Wilson for her excellent food styling and for being an absolute pleasure to work with, Dan Jones for the beautiful photography, Liz Belton and Linda Pullin for the gorgeous prop styling, Maria Lee-Warren on the fabulous design and Gordana Simakovic on production.

Special thanks to Julia Charles, Leslie Harrington and Cindy Richards for all their stellar work and particular thanks to my brilliant editor, Stephanie Milner, for all her support and patience. And lastly, a huge hug of thanks must go to my family and friends for scoffing the test bakes and saving them from a sad rubbish bin fate. Thank you, thank you.